Love Without Borders

Love Without Borders

How Bold Faith Opens the Door
to Embracing the Unexpected

ANGELA BRANIFF

HarperOne

An Imprint of HarperCollinsPublishers

HarperOne

FIRST EDITION

Library of Congress Cataloging-in-Publication Data

Names: Braniff, Angela, author.
Title: Love without borders : how bold faith opens the door to embracing the
    unexpected / Angela Braniff.
Description: First edition. I San Francisco : HarperOne, 2020.
Identifiers: LCCN 2019035476 (print) I LCCN 2019035477 (ebook) I ISBN
    9780062936264 (hardcover) I ISBN 9780062936271 (ebook)
Subjects: LCSH: Braniff, Angela. I Christian biography. I
    Mothers—Religious life.
Classification: LCC BR1725.B68255 A3 2020 (print) I
    LCC BR1725.B68255 (ebook) I DDC 277.308/3092 [B]—dc23
LC record available at https://lccn.loc.gov/2019035476
LC ebook record available at https://lccn.loc.gov/2019035477

20 21 22 23 24 LSC 10 9 8 7 6 5 4 3 2

Only by His grace, all for His glory.

To my family—
I will always strive to love you better,
but please know
I couldn't possibly love you more.

Contents

1. A Day in the Life   1

2. The Checklist Life   11

3. Our Meet Cute   23

4. A Mother Is Born   33

5. Dear God, Break My Heart   47

6. Kol Demama Daka   53
   THE STILL, SMALL VOICE

7. Moved to Action   57

8. Written in the Sand   63

9. This Is Africa   67

10. Fight, Flight, Freeze   79

11. Everything Changed   85
    ONE WORLD, TWO TRUTHS

CONTENTS

12. When the Door Closes   95

13. Jehovah Jireh   107

14. Infertility Begins   119

15. Our Rose   129

16. On Being Brave   139

17. Just One More . . .   151

18. Seeing Double   161

19. My Hallelujah Song   175

20. Belonging   191

Acknowledgments   *207*
Resources   *211*

Love Without Borders

1

A Day in the Life

This act of mothering is my worship to Him right now;
dying to self and delighting in them. There is failure.
Oh yes. It is messy and sloppy sometimes; yet,
[there is] forgiveness and grace and growing.

—Lovelyn Palm

Picture this: Outside the birds are chirping, the sun is peeking out over the trees in a blaze of orange glory, the smell of freshly brewed coffee permeates your entire house. The kids are happily playing together upstairs, and you're sitting on a plush couch, fuzzy blanket draped across your lap, reading your Bible and praying in peace and quiet.

It sounds beautiful doesn't it?

Well, that's about as far from my reality as you can get (*insert the sound of a record scratching here*).

If I could invite you into my house for a day, this is what you'd witness: I wake up abruptly because I've just been elbowed in the throat by a toddler—wait, make that two toddlers. As I throw back the covers I discover that those "leakproof" diapers are not, in fact, leakproof. I remove the sheets and add washing them to my already overflowing to-do list for the day. I can hear the loud, gleeful screams of my two boys running around the playroom. They've been up since at least 5:30 a.m., and I'm convinced they are a part of some kind of science experiment to test how little sleep a human can actually survive on. I make my way to the kitchen and brew what is destined to be the first of many cups of coffee for the day. And I pray—a lot!

My husband, CR, is downstairs getting this crazy train moving on out of the station. Last year we both became work-from-home parents, after CR left his corporate career of thirteen years to become a stay-at-home dad. Now, we work together as a team to keep my business and our family of nine functioning. Some days it's seamless, and some days it's madness.

The next hour or two is a flurry of bottles, diapers, scrambled eggs, more coffee, feeding the pets, loading the dishwasher, brushing teeth, and did I mention *more coffee?* It's a bit like herding cats to get everyone where they need to be.

The only thing I have left to do is to dress the twins. They're twenty months old and it's a bit of a rodeo. One minute they're cackling and laughing while you attempt to fit their squirmy little legs into pants, and the next they're crying and slapping at you because it's been twenty seconds, and they are over it now. Toddlers are nature's most fickle creatures, which is why God makes them so freakin' cute. He knows they need those big saucer eyes and sweet squeaky voices to survive.

I send one of the younger kids up to third floor to wake up my two oldest daughters. They are twelve and ten years old, and those girls love to sleep! I swear they'd sleep in until noon if I let them.

We homeschool, and so once all the kids are gathered together, we start the morning with some worship music and pray together, while the kids draw or paint in their Bible journals. Then we get started on the rest of our schoolwork. On a successful day, you might find Kennedy, my oldest daughter, doing her math on the computer, and CR at the kitchen table role-playing social stories with Rosie, our seven-year-old daughter, who has Down syndrome. In the study room Shelby, our ten-year-old daughter, would be devouring a new book series, and Jonah, our five-year-old son, might be with me in the schoolroom doing his alphabet flash cards. A quick peek around the corner and you'd find the twins are corralled in the living room riding around on their little scooters, and Noah, our seven-year-old, is practicing handwriting at the coffee table.

On another day, you may find all hell has broken loose: the twins are wearing only diapers, the kids are watching an animal documentary so we can call it "school," I'm up to my elbows in work to get done, and CR's shampooing carpets because, well, we have seven kids, two dogs, three cats, and something is always dirty. I like to think of these as "spice up your life" kind of days. Those crazy days when it seems the wheels have come off: we call those *spicy* days!

We wrap up our schoolwork before lunchtime, because afternoon is when my workday begins. I make videos on YouTube and write a blog, which has given me so much fulfillment and allowed me to share my passions with an incredible community online. My work has opened doors to opportunities I never knew would be possible, such as working with the brand that wants to partner with me to throw a "moms' night out" event for local foster moms who need to get a break and just be loved on. I'm humbled and amazed that I get to do this for a living!

When it's a filming day, I need to pull myself together a bit. Most days that means I apply fifty pounds of dry shampoo, a full-coverage concealer, and what I like to refer to as my "mullet outfit." You know how they say a mullet haircut is "business in the front and party in the back"? Yeah, that's my outfit. A cute shirt and earrings on the top and old ratty sweatpants on the bottom. I set up my lighting, make sure I have all my notes for the video, and gather the products I need. I'm ready to roll.

No sooner do I hit the record button than I hear crying coming from downstairs. I know CR is down there with the kids, but sometimes Mama just needs to make sure everything is okay. I run downstairs to do a quick well check and find the twins both in full meltdown mode. They are in the worst stage of toddlerhood right now: *the biting stage*. Neither twin has enough of a vocabulary to effectively communicate with each other, so when one of them takes a toy, the other retaliates by biting. I consider myself pretty well versed in parenting toddlers at this point, but having twins has ushered in a whole wave of issues that are totally new to me, and their constantly biting each other is definitely one of them. CR and I each grab a baby and attempt to comfort them. Luckily at this age, they are quick to forgive, and they are back to playing together in no time.

I rush back upstairs, but I'm already behind schedule. I hop onto another call to discuss the itinerary for a trip I'm taking to Uganda in a few weeks. This particular organization is working to empower vulnerable women in their local community by setting them up with dignified work and helping them to send their kids to school. The organization asked me to come to Uganda to see firsthand the work being done and the lives being changed; then I will share what I've seen with my amazing online community. When the call is over, it's time to sit back down in front of the camera and attempt to film again. Before I even get settled, I hear Rosie's little voice, "Hi, Mom! Whatcha doing?"

Rosie always seems to know when I'm filming something, and she loves to be on camera. She usually decides this is a great time for her daily chat. She asks me fifty questions about everything from my nail polish color to the lighting setup. She knows most of the answers already, since filming is a regular occurrence in our home, but I appease her and answer all her questions again. I'm just happy to hear her speaking in full sentences and using words in the proper context. She was almost five years old when we adopted her from China, and we had no idea how long it would take her to learn English. Down syndrome was totally new to us and we tried to have very few expectations of her.

It's now been three years since she came home, and I'm sitting here listening to her monologue about her brothers fighting downstairs and how Ivy fell down; Rosie wraps it up by asking me for a snack. I may have one hundred little things on my to-do list for that day, but I'll never grow tired of basking in utter gratitude for how far this girl has come and how she's changed my life forever. But, alas, there's still work to do. I usher her downstairs to grab a quick snack and then head back up to *finally* film my video.

Dinnertime is when the real show begins. The last few hours before bedtime are like the wild wild West around here; it's every man for himself, and I always just hope we all make it out alive. About the time the dinner table is set, I look out the back window to see my boys perched atop the roof of their two-story playhouse, singing silly songs and laughing. Honestly, I always thought people who had "wild" boys were just being bad parents. I'd roll my eyes when my sister's two boys would run around like little mongooses and think to myself, "If I ever have a boy, he's not going to behave like that." *Ha!*

Fast-forward six years, and now my two boys are twenty-five feet in the air, mere seconds from breaking an arm or a leg and laughing like hyenas. I inhale deeply as I head out into the yard to corral them in for dinner. I throw my hands on my hips and fuss, "Have you *no* sense of self-preservation?!" and they run cackling into the house for dinner.

When my boys were babies, as I rocked them to sleep, I'd pray over them. I'd beg God to help me be a good mom to boys; this was all new to me, and I had no idea what I was doing. I'd pray about their futures, what it would be like for them, as black boys to grow up with a white mom. I knew there was so much we'd need to learn together, and the responsibility weighed heavily on my heart. Would I be able to help them navigate this uncertain world we live in? I had more questions than answers, and all I knew for sure was that these were my boys, and I loved them fiercely.

Now the boys are seven and five years old, and while these prayers are still in my heart and mind every single day, they get pushed to the background of praying I can keep them alive on a day-to-day basis. Let's just say, they keep me young and give me gray hair, simultaneously.

When dinner is done, it's all hands on deck as we get everyone bathed and ready for bed. Kennedy and Shelby are my right-hand ladies. They were always wonderful big sisters, but when the twins were born it was as if the girls transformed into little mamas. They would beg me to let them change diapers and burp babies and even wanted to wear the twins in baby carriers around the house when they were fussy. These two really are such incredible kids, and CR and I are grateful they enjoy helping us when the night-time chaos ensues.

In this house we do what I call a "fast bath." That means you jump in the shower, wash your body and your hair, and you jump right back out. I'm talking in and out in less than three minutes. With two showers and nine people, we've mastered the art of the "fast bath." Jonah is my firecracker at this time of night, running naked up and down the hall-way so that I have to chase him around just to get some pants on him. This nightly streaking usually gets the rest of the kids howling with laughter, which only makes him faster and harder to catch. Once the wild J-man has finally been caught, lotioned, and put in bed, CR makes the final rounds of getting everyone tucked in.

When the lights are finally out, prayers have been said, and the noise level has decreased to almost nonexistent, CR and I flop down on the sofa to connect with each other at the end of a hectic day. We have a little mantra in our house, "Hard isn't always bad." Even as we drag our ex-hausted selves up the stairs to go to bed, we do it with happy hearts, knowing that being in this crazy story is ex-actly where we belong.

I know it sounds nuts, and to be honest, I probably would have laughed in your face if you had told me fourteen years ago, before I walked down the aisle, that I was about to embark on this incredible adventure and have seven kids; homeschool all of them; adopt from Africa, China, and the

United States; adopt a child with Down syndrome; give birth to twins that we adopted as embryos. . . . I mean, I'm not so sure I would have said, "Yes, sign me up for that!" It sounds like a reality show, not a real person's life. But that's the funny thing about God and the lives He calls us to. He really doesn't care if His call fits into your own life plans or follows the current cultural norms.

He just wants us to lay it all down and follow Him into the unknown. For me, following Him looks like listening to *kol demama daka*, which translated means "the sound of thin silence." Isn't that beautiful? It's the small, quiet whisper of God; when I'm listening, it guides me in the right direction.

For a long time, I thought the "right direction" meant following a checklist: Go to school. Check. Get married. Check. Get pregnant and have a child. Check. Buy a house. Check, check, check.

I did it all and was living the dream, but it wasn't God's dream for me. It wasn't until God started to break me open and show me all the ways He wanted me to live outside that checklist, to live outside the bounds of what we consider "normal," that I started to see begin to unfold a life more beautiful than I could have imagined. When I responded with a bold yes to what God put before me, my whole world changed.

The journey has not been easy or glamorous; it's been filled with ups and downs, highs and lows. Through it all, I've learned God's love knows no boundaries, so I want my love to have no borders. It took many years, and I still don't always get it right, but I finally quit trying to fit my life into a perfectly appointed little box and started striving every day not just to be willing to do what God asks of me, but to listen to Him eagerly, waiting for the next open door He places in my path. And as I follow this path, I find I become more and more the person He created me to be: a woman who isn't perfect or Super Mom, who is a bit weird, even—I mean, Dolly Parton is my hero, and I basically have the same sense of humor as a teenage boy. But there's so much beauty in being secure in who God created me to be: no boxes, no checklists—just me. It's easy to see and appreciate the diversity in His creation when we look at wildflowers, or a canopy of trees, or the abundance of creatures that He has designed. But, as humans, we tend to seek after more things that make us the same, rather than different. We are just as diverse and magnificent as any of His other creations, and I'm learning every day to appreciate what makes me unique.

I don't know what your life looks like, what path you are on, or what open doors you are facing. But my hope is that as you read my story you'll see the incredible things God can do when we break ourselves open and say yes to His quiet whisper.

2

The Checklist Life

When my heart is overwhelmed, lead me
to the rock that is higher than I.

—Psalm 61:2 (ASV)

Can I just be candid with y'all? As a kid and young adult, I had *no earthly clue* who I was, what I was good at, or what I wanted to do with my life. I never really stopped to consider what I enjoyed or what made my heart sing. I paid attention only to what others wanted from me or for me.

I have an older sister, Ashleigh; we are only thirteen months apart, which did not happen on purpose, according to my parents. (I vaguely remember a story about a dog chewing on the condom packaging, but don't hold me to that.) As close in age as my sister and I are, you'd think we would have had a ton of things in common as kids, but we were as different as could be. Ashleigh was this adorable, blond-haired, brown-eyed, vivacious baby genius, and I was, well . . . the opposite. I had green eyes and "dishwater" hair—you know, not really blond but not brown either; the color of water in the sink after you let the dishes "soak" (attractive, right?). I was quiet and shy and wasn't exactly a baby Einstein.

My parents entered Ashleigh in baby beauty pageants, which naturally she won. She had her name engraved on trophies that stood taller than her and received tiaras that glittered like a real crown fit for a princess. I never competed in pageants, not because I was so hideous that my parents kept me locked in a dungeon or anything, but I was just so painfully shy. I would have likely peed my pants or run off stage crying. I did a lot of crying as kid, so much crying that I earned the nickname "Angie Crybaby." I would turn into a puddle if someone looked at me wrong or, God forbid, my dad raised his voice. I think it's safe to say I wasn't pageant material.

Ashleigh wasn't just a pretty toddler; she was smart as a whip, too. In preschool, the teacher told my mom how Ashleigh would painstakingly place her macaroni in just the right spot, paying close attention to detail in order to form the perfect number two. She would even stay in from recess to ensure her macaroni number was glued to perfection. Meanwhile I was off somewhere eating crayons.

Make no mistake, my parents never hovered over me

wagging their fingers and saying, "Ashleigh is a genius, and you're stupid!" But even as a child, you can pick up on the things your parents *don't* say just as much as the things they do say. I quickly discovered I wasn't at the same level as Ashleigh when it came time for me to learn to read. Ashleigh had been reading for as long as I could remember, which makes sense because she taught herself to read at age four. Yep, she didn't just learn to read at a young age but actually taught herself.

I taught myself many things, too—you know, like how to do a somersault, or how to tackle my dad for a World Wrestling Federation–style throw-down in the living room after dinner, or how to hide my half-chewed food in a napkin and flush it down the toilet when my mom forced me to eat hamburger patties smothered in gravy. I did all those things quite well, but I certainly wasn't teaching myself to read at the ripe old age of four.

Even so, kindergarten was surprisingly fun for me. I made friends, played games, and paid zero attention to the fact that I wasn't really learning anything. The end of the year came, and I remember taking some tests, but my mom never said anything, so I just assumed all was well. Sure, I wasn't reading, but I was too busy chasing butterflies and sharing cookies to worry about something as trivial as reading.

First grade rolled around and my lack of interest in learning began to cause some problems. I was confused by most of what my teacher was saying, so I just made casual conversation with the kids around me. My teacher would then stop her instruction to fuss at me, and of course the sheer embarrassment of being reprimanded in front of the whole class would keep me quiet for a while, but then I'd grow increasingly bored again and start chatting up my neighbor. I never wanted to get in trouble, and Lord knows I didn't want my teacher not to like me, but it was almost compulsory: I *needed* to talk, move, and wiggle in my seat.

My report cards would always say things like this:

"Angie is a sweet girl, but she needs to be less social in class."

"Angie talks *too* much!"

And then, after most of the class had far surpassed me in skills and knowledge, the teacher's notes shifted focus and had a more concerned tone:

"Angie still can't read, I think she may be dyslexic."

"Perhaps, if you get her glasses, that will help her learn to read."

As it turns out, my mom had been trying to get me into special classes for extra help in reading but was told I couldn't be fit in until third grade. That response was unacceptable to my mom, and she became increasingly frustrated with our little school. Eventually, she decided to pull me out and began teaching me at home. While I fully understand and agree with her decision now, at the time, I felt like a colossal failure. All I could think was, "I'm *so dumb* that I can't even be in a regular school!"

My mom was right, which is not unusual, and I learned

to read fairly quickly after we started homeschooling. Turns out, I just needed the information presented in a different way. We also were able to get our schoolwork done in just a few hours each day, which left plenty of time to play outside, use my imagination, and burn off energy. Who had time to sit at a desk for hours on end anyway? I had a rock family in the backyard that needing tending, a river made from chocolate that needed stirring, and a roller-skating routine that needed some final choreographic touches. My brain did much better in school when it got lots of time *not* doing school.

Like most children, I was seeking an anchor, the thing that connected me without question to my family. I think it's ingrained in us to look for those commonalities; they help us find our identity and feel like we belong.

In my family, I saw the "genius gene" make its way from my grandfather, to my mother, to my sister. Papa Jim, my mom's dad, worked for NASA during the Saturn program and spent the rest of his career rising through the ranks at IBM. He did all of this after marrying my grandma when they were just sixteen and eighteen years old. They even had their first child, my aunt Debbie, shortly after getting married.

That "genius gene" was then passed down to my mother. Aptitude testing in fifth grade revealed what a smart cookie she was. Over the summer, she was invited to the university to take some college-level classes with a handful of other young brainiacs. Like many highly intelligent kids, she was bored in school and did what was needed to graduate high school a year early. She could have done anything she wanted, but college wasn't really seen as a priority for women at that time, so she never went.

I watched as the "genius gene" made its way to my sister; clearly, the apple doesn't fall far from the tree. Looking at my family tree, I couldn't shake the feeling that maybe I wasn't even an apple—maybe I was an orange or something?

I did take after someone in my family though: my dad. He would try to encourage me with stories of how things weren't always easy for him either. He'd talk about grit, hard work, integrity, and character.

My dad has a work ethic that is unrivaled by most. He was only twelve years old when he got his first job delivering the morning paper before school. By fifteen he was working at the local gas station, and as soon as he had a driver's license, he took the breakfast shift at Hardy's before heading to class. His dream was to be a fighter pilot, like his uncle Buddy, but because my dad was legally blind without his glasses, flying was out of the question. He'd considered many other professions that interested him, such as being a lawyer, but his father insisted that Dad go to school for engineering, based on his natural ability to fix things. He loved working on cars and could tinker with the best of 'em. But my dad hated math and science so, as you might imagine, college-level math as an engineering major was not easy; he ended up dropping out.

My parents, like theirs before them, married young and

started a family young. My mom was eighteen when she had Ashleigh and nineteen when she had me. Money was tight, and my dad found himself, once again, throwing papers at 3 a.m. before heading into a full day of work. Heck, my mom even took a paper route in the afternoons to help make ends meet. My parents were resilient, determined, and hardworking.

My dad's willingness to do whatever it took to care for his family led us to move roughly a million times. Shortly after mom pulled me out of school, we moved to a little gray ranch-style house in North Carolina, and that is where I met our neighbor Sabrina. She was around my parents' age and was unlike anyone I'd ever met. She was loud, hilarious, and totally unbuttoned. Her three little kids were wild and fun, just like their mom. My mother was always very buttoned-up and proper. She raised us to be polite, obedient, perhaps even a bit reserved. Sabrina, however, gave off a serious hippie vibe, and I *loved* it!

Being around Sabrina ignited a part of my brain I didn't even really know existed. She taught our whole family how to lighten up—not with any direct lessons or pointed conversations, but just by being herself. Her free spirit made us feel free, too. I became more relaxed and soon found that when I let myself say my thoughts out loud, people would laugh. I didn't even really know then what sarcasm was, but apparently I was fluent.

Sabrina had given me a newfound confidence and helped me unearth my inner comedian, so at family get-togethers, I stopped being so meek and began firing back at my uncles when they aimed their jokes at me. Of course, as a small kid, my jokes usually had to do with my uncles' beer bellies or receding hairlines. It wasn't comedy gold, but it made the adults laugh, nonetheless.

The first time I joked this way with my uncles, I sort of held my breath and waited to see whether my parents would scold me for talking that way. Being respectful was a big deal in our house. We were from the South; you always said "Yes, ma'am" or "No, sir," and you never called an adult by his or her first name but instead said "Mr. Jones" or "Mrs. Smith." My mother would have laid me out if I had ever been rude to an adult. So this was new territory for me. I was swimming in unfamiliar waters here, hoping not to get sucked under by the rules of etiquette. A quick glance in my dad's direction revealed a Cheshire cat grin.

He was proud.

I think my family just enjoyed seeing me come out of my shell. Instead of hiding my tears behind the sleeve of my neon-colored windbreaker, I was confidently interacting with people. Seeing this might have even been a relief to my family. At that point they were probably saving up to purchase the bubble "Angie Crybaby" was going to need to protect her from the cruel world she was obviously so unable to navigate. I don't think they really cared about *The Southern Girl's Guide to Etiquette* so much anymore; they were just happy to see me step out from the shadows a bit.

Turns out, I wasn't just funny; I had a quick wit, too. Humor and sarcasm became my shield. I learned that they had value beyond just making those around me laugh. I could use humor to mask hurt feelings, insecurity, and vulnerability, too. If someone said something that hurt my feelings, I'd just make a joke about it.

Oh, that "Angie Crybaby" was still in there, but I discovered humor as a way to keep her silenced. It didn't really matter whether what the person said actually hurt my feelings or not, so long as people never knew things got to me.

By the time high school rolled around, I'd spent so much time in preservation mode trying to make everyone happy that I was utterly lost, not knowing who I was at all. I didn't have too hard of a time staying out of trouble because at least I had a clear compass on right and wrong. The few times I did find myself hanging out with the "bad girls," I'd panic and just call my mom to come get me before I could do anything all that bad. I knew where I *didn't* belong; my problem was not knowing where I *did*.

I wasn't really an athlete, but I tried softball to make my dad happy. I wasn't a cheerleader, but I did Pop Warner in eighth grade to make my mom happy. I wasn't a dancer, but I tried out for dance team my freshman year to make my friend happy. All this uncertainty and people-pleasing made it hard for me to even know who I really was, let alone form healthy friendships with other girls my age.

The boxes start at a pretty young age, don't they? You've got to fit into one of them to belong anywhere. Are you an athlete? Are you a theater kid? Are you a nerd? Are you a goth kid? It seems so silly when you think about it, but it's just as pervasive in adulthood, too. There are boxes for everything from your style of parenting (free-range, attachment, strict) to the way you decorate your home (modern, farmhouse, traditional), the career path you've chosen (working mom, stay-at-home mom, mom with a side hustle), and even the type of church you go to (hipster, mega, old-school). The boxes never seem to end and seem to be how we identify with one another and attempt to find like-minded people so we can form a posse of stay-at-home moms who like shiplap walls and co-sleeping.

I found myself desperate to fit in somewhere but didn't feel at home anywhere. When I looked to the future, I became even more lost. My sister had dreams of having a family and being a mom, but I wasn't even sure I liked kids! If only I had known then that someday I would have enough kids to create my own Little League team. . . . Yet another reason I can fully attest that God's plans are so much better than our own. But I digress.

Beyond not knowing whether I wanted to have kids, all I heard growing up was people dismissing my sister's dreams of motherhood, asking her why she didn't want to "do more with her life." I internalized the belief that doing something meaningful with my life meant I needed to have a high-powered career. Being "just a mom" wasn't going to be enough. Around this time, my parents decided to grow our family, and my baby sister, Savannah, was born. Not only were Ashleigh and I crazy about her, but she softened my heart a little to the idea that I actually might want to have kids of my own someday. Savannah was thirteen years younger than me, and she became like our real-life baby doll. For Ashleigh, this experience only solidified her desire to be a mom, but for me, it wasn't so simple.

I didn't know who I was. I didn't know what I wanted or what I was passionate about. And instead of digging deep to figure that out or turning to God in prayer to ask what He wanted for my life, I turned to what other people around me were saying and doing to build my checklist life.

The worst part was that I bought the lie that if I just checked all the boxes and did everything "right," I'd be happy:

Get good grades.

Go to church every Sunday.

Be respectful to teachers.

Make your parents proud.

That's the recipe, right? That's all you need. Be the good Christian girl, make the "right" choices, and you'll be fulfilled. Obviously, none of the aforementioned things is bad—they are all good things. But it wasn't healthy to fill my plate with things that I thought would make people like me or love me.

I've seen this checklist mentality pop up throughout my

adult life, too. If I could just find the recipe for making the right choices, then I'd be fulfilled:

Get married.

Buy a house.

Have two kids, maybe three, but no more.

And so on.

It took me thirty-some years to realize that there is no formula to life—especially not the bold life that God is calling us to. When God calls us, He calls us to dreams unimaginable. It's never the same for any two people. We all have different paths to walk, and some are perhaps bolder and crazier-looking than others, but the point is that we are meant to be guided by God, by His unique story for each us, and not by a checklist.

Eventually, I'd get there. It would take time, as well as a major meltdown and a whole lot of on-my-knees, facedown, humbled kind of prayer, but I'd get there. In the meantime, I was about to meet the person who would change my life— the person who would make me feel seen and loved for who I really was, not who I thought I should be.

3

Our Meet Cute

Love is friendship that has caught fire.

—Ann Landers

I met CR in a very typical "boy meets girl" kind of way. To hear him tell it, though, it was an epic love story for the ages. After finishing eighth grade, a bunch of my friends went to hang out at a local pizza place. I was sitting at a table picking pepperoni off my slice and sipping Dr Pepper when CR came in with his best friend, Aaron. He says he took one look at me, leaned over to Aaron, and whispered, "That's the girl I'm going to marry!"

I'd like to tell you that the feeling was mutual; however, for me, he was just another boy in a crowd of cracking voices, sweaty palms, and braces. We were thirteen, so I wasn't exactly looking for Mr. Right yet.

We did become fast friends, though. Over the next few years, we spent a lot time together, and I always knew he was different from the other boys. He was kind and compassionate, and he treated the girls he dated with respect. Our friendship grew stronger during the awkward high school years.

At the end of my junior year, my parents announced we were moving all the way across the country to North Carolina. In the days before social media, my friends and I knew it was unlikely we'd stay in one another's lives after such a big move. It was the fear of never seeing me again that drove CR to finally share his feelings. One day after school, I found a note flapping around under my windshield wiper—a love note, to be exact. The note went on for pages and pages, filled with all the details of how CR knew I was the one and couldn't let me move away without telling me. He wasn't begging me to be his girlfriend or anything; he just needed me to know that he had loved me for all these years from afar, and the thought of never seeing me again was enough to give him the courage to finally tell me how he felt.

I knew he had poured his heart out into this note, but initially I felt annoyed, maybe even a little angry. I mean, I was moving away in just a few weeks! I had never thought of him that way, and I felt he was going to ruin our friendship. Of course, I'd always thought he was cute and funny and a nice guy, but I'd watched him date other girls, and we had always just had each other in what I assumed was the "friend zone." Could I like him as more than a friend? After taking a little time to examine my feelings, I figured, "Why the heck not? I've only got a few more weeks here in Oregon, let's just see how it goes. If it's a dumpster fire, then I'll just slip away to North Carolina and start a whole new life, and no one will be the wiser."

We started dating and, to my surprise, it wasn't a disaster; in fact, it was kind of a fairy tale. Once I allowed myself to think about him in a different way, as more than just a friend, I saw a whole new side of him that I had never known. We became inseparable over the weeks that followed. All the wonderful characteristics I'd seen in him as a friend were amplified, and I found myself falling for him hard and fast!

When school let out for the year, we said our teary—and incredibly overly dramatic—goodbyes, and I flew to North Carolina, where I was supposed to start a whole new life. However, I didn't last long in North Carolina. I told my parents I missed my friends, wanted to finish out my senior year, *blah blah blah*—but really, I missed CR. (Sorry, Mom and Dad.)

Eventually my parents agreed to let me move back to Oregon, live with a friend, and finish my senior year there. CR and I were thrilled to be back together again. The entire year was great: I landed a coveted internship at Intel, hung out with friends, kept my grades up, and had a boyfriend

I was madly in love with. Life seemed pretty grand. Then came graduation. CR went off to college in California, and I moved all the way across the country back to North Carolina to attend college near my parents.

Have you ever looked in the mirror and not recognized the person staring back at you? That's how I felt on my first day of college. I'd spent extra time fixing my hair, doing my makeup just right, and picking out the perfect outfit to start this new chapter. I looked like a successful college student on the outside, but on the inside, it was a different story.

I had no clue what I was going to major in, I had exactly zero friends, no job, nothing. It felt like I was invisible, like people just walked through me as I strolled from class to class. I tried, I really did, but the lectures felt like torture, and even the assignments seemed silly and insignificant. I wanted to stay focused on the long-term goal of getting a college degree, but I didn't like it. Not any of it.

Meanwhile, I'd talk to my boyfriend and hear all about how he was living the full college life on the beautiful beaches of Malibu, California, while I was stuck in bug-infested, hotter-than-the-surface-of-the-sun North Carolina. At least, that's how I saw things at the time. CR and I made the long-distance thing work for only a few months before the inevitable happened and we put an end to our romantic relationship. Because our relationship was built on a friendship first, we both agreed to find a way to salvage the friendship and agreed to keep in touch as best as we could.

We remained such good friends, in fact, that over the next three years CR listened as I whined about a new guy I was dating or cried about a recent breakup. He was there for me even when it must have been so painful for him. Every time I'd ask him about girls he liked or was dating, he would always brush it off and tell me, "There's just no one like you."

I mean, smooth. Real smooth, buddy.

I continued my quest to find my place in this world by enrolling in nursing school at my mom's suggestion. Over the next few years I worked full-time and went to school full-time, and even though I was working toward a good job, with great pay and flexibility, I still just wasn't where I felt I belonged—where I felt I fit. I'd even finally made new friends, and yet I still felt unseen. I was doing all the "right" things, but the hole still gaped open inside me.

During that time, CR stayed in touch through email and the occasional phone call. Eventually, he asked whether he could fly me out to visit him for the new year. He had transferred schools and was living back in Oregon now. I was reluctant, but since I knew I'd also get to see Ashleigh, I agreed.

On my flight out, I gave myself all the tough-girl "You don't need no man" pep talks and armed myself with every logical reason why we should *not* get back together—the major one being that he lived three thousand miles away, and long-distance relationships just don't work. Long distance hadn't worked for us before; what would be different this time?

After a six-hour flight, I landed in the Portland airport and made my way down to baggage claim. I immediately saw CR waiting for me. He'd put on about twenty-five pounds of muscle since the last time I'd seen him, and I am not afraid to tell you that this independent, single-by-choice lady became weak in the knees and red-faced. Dear God, what had he been doing since we parted ways? I mean, he was always "boy next door" cute, but now . . . this was not good.

I played it cool, gave him a friendly hug—you know the kind, where you're sure to leave room for the Holy Spirit, a youth pastor–approved kind of hug—and pretended not to notice his new physique.

The next few days are kind of a blur. We hadn't seen each other in three years, and yet it was like I'd never left. Everything felt so effortless, natural, and comfortable. I know for many people that feeling of "home" is a place they love, but for me that feeling of "home" was a person, and I was finally realizing that. CR was my happy place: the place where I felt seen, heard, and loved for exactly who I was, no strings attached. I didn't have to pretend to be perfect. I could be broken and, quite frankly, a hot mess, yet he still loved me.

I didn't have all the answers for my life. I didn't know what I was supposed to become or what my life was going to look like. But I knew one thing for sure: I wanted CR in it.

Over the next couple months, we spent countless hours on the phone. Many of those conversations brought us to the topic of marriage. I think we both knew, even in high school, that we wanted to spend our lives together. I'm hesitant to say "made for each other" or "meant to be" because I think that can detract from how much work marriage really is. But since we had been apart for a few years, when we did finally find our way back to each other, we knew it was for good this time.

I flew out to visit him in Portland a couple months later. This time, when CR was waiting for me in the baggage claim, he seemed nervous. I found it a little odd, thinking, "Come on, dude, you won me back. . . . What's with the nervous Nelly attitude?" Bags were coming around the carousel when I heard a quiet whisper pass through the crowd. Everyone was pointing at one gray baggage tray making its way around the conveyor belt. I stood up and peered into the tray to see what all the fuss was about. Inside was a single rose, and a card that said, "Angela."

It took me a second to realize I was the "Angela" it was for, but once it clicked I slid the box off the conveyor belt and turned around to find CR down on one knee. The entire baggage claim was full of people with their eyes fixed on us, oohing and aahing. I don't even really remember what CR said, I only heard the last part.

"Will you marry me?"

Feeling nervous but also confident, I said yes, and the airport erupted with cheers and applause. It was my own little fairy-tale moment.

A few months later, I dropped out of nursing school, quit my job, and moved to Oregon so we could get married. I turned twenty-one two weeks before the big day, and while I know that seems so young to get married, I never really thought much of it. As I mentioned earlier, I had heard stories all my life about the women in my family who married really young. I don't know if it was just the way it was "back then" or in the South perhaps, but my grandma was sixteen on her wedding day, my aunt was sixteen, my mom was eighteen when she married my dad, and even my older sister Ashleigh got married at seventeen. For my nineteenth birthday, my mom took me out to breakfast and she joked with me that when she was my age she was married with a baby and one on the way.

The idea of marrying CR when we were both twenty-one never concerned me or my family. I knew I wanted to be married, I knew I wanted to marry CR, the boy I'd been friends with for most my life and whom I loved deeply. It was simply the next step in achieving that elusive fulfillment I'd been searching for. Don't get me wrong: marrying CR was one of the best decisions I've ever made, and I'd do it again a million times over. But it was another methodical movement through my life—as if it was a board game and getting married would get me closer to winning.

Still, I was excited about starting my life with CR. Where everything else in my life felt uncertain, I felt certain about building a life with CR. I knew we were embarking on a great adventure together.

4

A Mother
Is Born

Making the decision to have a child is momentous.
It is to decide forever to have your heart go
walking around outside your body.

—Elizabeth Stone

When CR and I were dating, we often discussed what we envisioned our future family looking like. We talked about names we liked and the number of kids we'd have. We both laugh now when we think back to those conversations. CR was an only child, and he knew he definitely wanted us to have at least two kids, while I always thought maybe we'd have four kids. That seemed like a big number to both of us, but we loved the idea of having a "large" family. I had also shared with him that I would like to adopt at some point in my life. I had watched a documentary about adoption in high school, and from that point on, I knew it was something I wanted to explore and that whomever I married would have to at least be open to the conversation. CR was always an incredibly compassionate person, and I wasn't surprised when he agreed that adoption would be a great way to complete our family at some point. Like most young people, we had a lot of grand ideas of what our lives would be. We talked and dreamed about dozens of scenarios, never really knowing which ones would eventually turn into reality.

We'd been married just ten months when I found out I was pregnant. CR was about to graduate college and already had a job lined up with a national bank. When I made the move back to Oregon, I was lucky enough to get a pretty amazing job writing marketing proposals for an engineering firm in Portland. Everything was going great. We both had great jobs, and now we were going to have a baby!

The tile floor was cold, but it honestly felt good. I found myself, once again, draped over the toilet like a wet blanket. I was not throwing up food; I hadn't eaten in days. It was just a green acid, with some blood mixed in. My body was getting a little more frail as the days wore on, and I began to wonder if this was really what morning sickness was supposed to be like.

My sister advised me to call my midwife, since this level of morning sickness just didn't seem normal to her. I'd had a quick appointment with the midwife at the very beginning to confirm the pregnancy, so when she opened the exam room door and saw me just a few weeks later looking frail and sickly, her face made it clear that something was wrong.

She told me I had something called hyperemesis gravidarum (HG), that it affects fewer than 3 percent of pregnant women, and that it basically meant I suffered from extreme vomiting and nausea. I knew something wasn't right, so I was relieved to have a diagnosis for what was happening to me. Unfortunately, the midwife also told me that there was no cure and not much could be done even to help alleviate the symptoms. She prescribed vitamin B6 and doxylamine, a sleep aid thought to help relieve nausea, and she also set me up to get regular intravenous infusions, since so much vomiting can lead to dehydration.

Unfortunately, none of these made me feel better. I spent my days lying on my sister's couch, watching the Food Network on television (because when you can't eat it's fun to watch other people cook and eat), and throwing up fifteen to twenty times a day. I had taken all my vacation days at work, which meant I would likely lose my job before I could go back, and CR was just starting his new job at the bank. We didn't know when I was going to get better, and we needed a plan to move out of my sister's tiny apartment. Ashleigh and I began tossing around the idea of moving back to North Carolina, where our parents lived. Ash had a baby now and was longing to raise him near our folks, and now I was going to have a baby soon enough, and the cost of living was so much better there. We discussed it with our husbands and were a bit surprised that they were totally on board with the idea!

CR was able to transfer his job with the bank, and when I was sixteen weeks pregnant we made our way three thousand miles across the country to plant our roots in North Carolina.

We moved in with my parents while CR got his new job under way, and I searched for a new doctor in the area. I reached out to a few local friends, got some recommendations, and began calling around. I had all my previous files mailed to the new clinic and went in for my first appointment at about twenty weeks. The doctor looked confused as she read my chart, glancing up at me every few seconds, seemingly perplexed.

"Is this correct? You've lost nearly thirty pounds so far this pregnancy?" As I explained to her all that had happened over the past few months, I realized that I had gotten so used to throwing up every day, not eating much, and being miserable, that I hadn't fully grasped what a bad situation this was. She let me know that I was at a point in my pregnancy where I really should be gaining weight, and that over the next few weeks we'd be doing some tests and ultrasounds to check on the baby.

I was out one afternoon running errands with my mom and she wanted to get some food at Chick-fil-A. She asked if I wanted to just *try* and eat something, so I agreed to give it a shot and ordered some chicken nuggets and a sweet tea. Y'all, it was one of the few times in six months that I had been able to keep some real food down! Now I believe it really is the Lord's food—no one will ever convince me otherwise. The good news was that I finally found something I could eat; the bad news was that it was the *only* thing I could eat. I probably ate more than a thousand chicken nuggets over the coming months, and we actually nicknamed the baby "Nugget." The nickname stuck after she was born, too, at least for a little while.

Slowly and steadily, I started to put some weight back on. We'd made it almost to thirty weeks, and everything was looking pretty good. Around this time, my uncle Buddy passed away, and I wanted to go down to South Georgia for the funeral service. I assured my mom I was healthy enough to travel, and so we started making plans to go. Buddy was actually my dad's uncle, but I called him Uncle Buddy, too. He was as sarcastic as they came, a former fighter pilot, and I remember he had a life-size cutout of Elvira in his garage. He was a character if there ever was one and one of my all-time favorite people. There was little that could keep me from paying my respects to him and all he'd done for our country.

Down in Georgia, Mom and I stayed at Geema's (my dad's mom) house, and I rode to the funeral with my dad's brother and his girlfriend. We all said our goodbyes, cried, and laughed through tears at the funny stories his lifelong friends told. As I made my way back to my uncle's car, I started getting a shooting pain in my side. It was a totally new sensation and, frankly, it scared me a little. The drive back to Geema's was only twenty minutes but it felt like hours. The pain was increasing, and I felt myself getting panicky. Mom was already back at the house when I arrived, and so I described all my symptoms to her hoping she'd know what might be happening. I kept wondering whether this could be early labor, but I was only thirty weeks pregnant.

I took an over-the-counter urinary tract infection medication and cranberry juice at my mom's suggestion, and this eased the pain enough that I could sleep that night. The next morning I was feeling a smidge better, so we felt pretty confident about making the five-hour drive back up to North Carolina.

We were about an hour from home when the pain started again. That shooting pain I felt was replaced with an excruciating stabbing feeling. It was all I could do to keep from crying out. I put all my weight on the opposite side, shifted in my seat, drank fluids, and prayed like I never had before. True to my people-pleasing nature, I never wanted to inconvenience anyone, and I knew my folks were tired from the trip and wanted to go home so I tried to just grin and bear it. But after a while the pain became too much to bear, and

I asked my mom to take me to urgent care. Something was wrong and I felt like I needed to be seen as soon as possible.

I was white-knuckled the rest of the drive back into Charlotte, and our first stop once we got into the city limits was at an urgent care clinic. The nurse practitioner took one look at me and said, "I'd bet you have a kidney stone."

She said there wasn't much they could do for me since I was pregnant, gave me some low-dose pain meds, and sent me home. I wasn't entirely satisfied with that answer, but there wasn't much else to be done. Many times, kidney stones will pass on their own in time, and the pain medication did seem to be taking the edge off.

It was approaching midnight when the meds wore off and the pain came back even stronger. I honestly didn't know there was a level of pain like this. I woke up CR and told him to take me to the emergency room. My mom came, too, and when we entered through the ER doors, the guy behind the counter thought I was in labor. I assured him I wasn't, but he sent me up to the labor and delivery department anyway. The doctor checked me to see whether I was in labor and, as I suspected, I was not. She ran tests and agreed that I must have a kidney stone.

This doctor gave me a much stronger dose of pain medication that worked wonders but also affected me in other, less helpful ways. My poor nurse experienced a very strange and not at all appropriate side of me. She was a sweet and soft-spoken young black girl, and I must have called her "girlfriend" and "sister" and "hunny" about forty times. She probably wanted to slap this ridiculous white girl, high on pain medication acting like a complete fool. Again, I thank the good Lord that social media didn't exist in the same ways back then, because I'm certain this could have been one of those viral video moments, like when kids get their wisdom teeth out and their parents film their absurd behavior. Man, it could have been really bad.

Being the kind-hearted woman she was, instead of punching me in the face, the nurse laughed. So did CR and my mom. I'm glad I could keep everyone entertained while we waited for a tech to get in to do my kidney ultrasound. It was the middle of the night by now, and this poor kid looked like he'd woken from the dead. Sure enough, he found a kidney stone—a *big* one. The doctor deemed it too big for me to pass on my own, and options for what to do from here were pretty limited since I was pregnant. Normally doctors would do something called lithotripsy to break the stone up so it could pass, but for what I hope are obvious reasons you can't shake up a pregnant lady.

The next best option was to place a stent, which basically creates space for the stone to pass. I was wheeled back to the operating room and put under anesthesia. The procedure was quick, but I remember upon waking, feeling so incredibly sore in my, ummm . . . lady bits. I barely cracked my eyes open and told the nurse it felt like I had just had sex with an elephant. She burst out laughing, and later that day my mom brought me a lovely bouquet of flowers from the gift shop and a small stuffed elephant. Very funny, Mom!

We were all hopeful that the stent would do its job, but after more than a week I was still in pain and there was no stone to be found in my cute little toilet hat. Another visit to the doctor, and the decision was made to place a nephrostomy tube. It's basically a small tube that goes through your back and directly into your kidney to drain it since the stone isn't allowing it to drain properly. With this procedure you also get a fun bag to carry around like a purse. A purse full of pee. I've always been a girl who loves accessories, namely purses, but this one wasn't exactly a new designer bag. Alas, if this procedure would help ease the pain, then I was happy to give it a shot!

The doctors felt that since putting me under full anesthesia the first time had "irritated" my uterus, causing some early contractions, this time they would use something called twilight sedation. I understood them to say that I wouldn't really feel anything, but that couldn't have been further from the truth. I was half awake during the procedure, and I remember moaning in pain as they pushed the tube through my side and into my kidney. Then they sewed it to skin to hold it in place. That was the worst part. I had never had stitches, so this was my first experience having my skin sewn. I was not a fan.

I wasn't coherent enough to talk though; I could only make low groans. The doctors finished up and moved me to the recovery room. I lay there, still unable to talk, as my mom and CR came in the room to check on me. The nurse boasted proudly to my mom, "She did great, she only cried out a few times!"

The look on my mom's face was a bit horrified and confirmed for me that we all had thought this "twilight sedation" would make the procedure painless—apparently not!

As luck would have it, the stent didn't fully solve the problem either, so at thirty-six weeks pregnant, the doctor decided my little nugget would be safer out than in, and once she was delivered they would be able to safely address my kidney issues. The doctor wanted to be sure the steroid shots I had been given weeks prior, to help the baby's lungs develop faster, had actually done their job, so the doctor sent me for an amniocentesis. Which is a fancy word for shoving a very long needle into your pregnant belly and pulling out amniotic fluid to test the baby's lung maturity. The procedure is not without risk, but we were at a point that the benefits outweighed that risk.

CR was working, so my mom came with me to this appointment. I could do little to hide my terror when the doctor entered the room to perform this procedure. We'd been sent to a specialty ultrasound clinic, so this fella was a new face for me. His attitude was a bit off-putting as he kept making it all seem like no big deal. My fear bubbled over into passive aggression when I told him how nervous I was and he replied, "It's fine—it doesn't really hurt that bad." Before I could filter myself, I snorted back, "Oh, really?

When was the last time you had this done?" My mom was fifty shades of embarrassed, and in hindsight I should have waited until after the doctor shoved the giant needle in my belly to act like such a brat.

He was sort of right—it wasn't that bad—but still, maybe he could have been a little less flippant to his patient, especially when he was speaking from *zero* personal experience. But I digress.

The results came back in just a few hours. The baby's lungs looked great, so an induction was set for the next day.

Kennedy Jayne Braniff came screaming into the world on January 10, 2007. She tipped the scales at a whopping five pounds, nine ounces, and for the first time, I felt like I was right where I was supposed to be. Gazing into her tiny blue eyes, I found a sense of belonging, meaning, and purpose. Life was no longer just about CR and myself, and I found such comfort in that. Now I had this little person, who was solely dependent on me for everything. Becoming a mom made me feel more like myself than I ever had before. It was as if the role of motherhood had always been out there, waiting for me to fill it.

Kennedy was barely one year old when we decided to try for another baby. We knew we wanted more children, and we hoped that my battle with hyperemesis in my first pregnancy was perhaps something that would happen only once.

Much to our shock, after just one month of trying, I found out I was pregnant again! Looking back, I don't think we even realized how lucky we were to conceive so quickly and easily. We were grateful to be pregnant, and our next step was to wait and see whether the sickness would return. The day I turned seven weeks pregnant, hyperemesis reared its ugly head. This time the doctors were more proactive and got me set up quickly with a home health nurse, a constant IV fluid drip, and even a medication pump to keep the Zofran (an antinausea medication) flowing through me twenty-four hours a day. It wasn't enough. I was losing weight quickly and, no matter how many meds were pumped through me, I couldn't keep anything down.

By my eleventh week of pregnancy the doctor decided I needed to have a peripherally inserted central catheter (PICC line) placed; this is a central line placed in your upper arm that runs through a large vein into your heart, helping the body absorb nutrition more effectively. I shuffled my way through the rest of my second pregnancy, never feeling fantastic, but doing better than I had with my first.

We found out at twenty weeks that this baby was going to be another girl! I was ecstatic! Truthfully, I was scared to have a boy. I'd grown up with a sister close in age, and I knew what a blessing that would be to my girls. Having a sister is like having a built-in best friend. Sure, there are years when you pull hair, name-call, and steal each other's clothes. But the years after that, the ones when you talk for hours, share every little detail, and are there for each other as you both become wives and mothers—those are the magical years. I really didn't know for sure at this point whether we'd ever have any more kids, so I was thankful my girls were going to have each other.

We began tossing around names, and one that I really loved was Reagan. CR quickly squashed that idea, since he was certain everyone would think we had some weird obsession with presidents if we had two girls named Kennedy and Reagan. With that name off the table, I immediately went back to one of my favorite names of all time, Shelby. *Steel Magnolias* is my all-time favorite movie; I've seen it so many times I could likely perform the whole thing for you, and I wouldn't miss a single line. Shelby's character, played by Julia Roberts, is smart, sassy, and strong-willed, all attributes I would love my daughter to have. CR agreed with my name suggestion, and on October 1, 2008, Shelby Darlene Braniff came fast and furiously into the world! She had a head covered with dark hair, completely contrasting with Kennedy, who was born mostly bald with a little bit of blond fuzz.

I often feel God reveals things to me through numbers and dates, so it warmed my heart when I realized the girls' birthdays were mirrors of each other: Kennedy born on 01/10 and Shelby on 10/01.

Up to this point in my life I'd felt a bit out of sorts, like I was not made for this world, because I had never felt like I belonged much of anywhere. But now I had an incredible husband who made me feel loved and seen for just being me, and I had two beautiful, healthy daughters who gave me a sense of purpose that I'd never had before.

They helped me see how little my life was actually about me, teaching me day by day that sacrifice is actually a good thing and that laying down my own selfishness to care for them would always be my highest calling. My heart had always felt a bit wild, a little unsteady, and now these little freckle-faced girls were taming it.

5

Dear God, Break My Heart

There is an instinct in a woman to love most her
own child—and an instinct to make any
child who needs her love, her own.

—Robert Brault

"What are we going to do with a five-bedroom house?" CR asked, chuckling. We had finally done it! Six years after we got married, we had two adorable little girls and now we had just signed on the dotted line to purchase our very first home. It was a few years after the big market crash, and the previous owners had abandoned the house more than a year earlier. It sat vacant as the bank continued to lower the price, month after month, in an attempt to unload the house from the bank's books. We had a front-row seat to watch the price drop, since the house was just down the street from my parent's home, and once the price hit a number we could afford, we decided to try to buy the house.

We hadn't been preparing to buy a house. We had no money saved for the down payment and honestly weren't really even completely sure we could afford the mortgage payment. It was quite a bit more than we'd been paying for rent, but something told us this place was meant to be ours. We sold anything that wasn't nailed down, desperate to get the money together. I sold furniture, clothes, and baby gear that was just gathering dust. CR sold vintage baseball cards, and we even went to both our grandparents and borrowed the last bit of money to cover the closing costs. We were tenacious and knew that this quest to become homeowners was really the last milestone on the way to achieving the American dream.

Not only were we able to buy the house, but because it was in foreclosure, we got an amazing deal, paying about half of what the house was worth. We haven't always made the best decisions with money, but *that* was a good one. The house, unsurprisingly, did need quite a bit of a work—such as figuring out how to turn the previous tenants' homemade sound studio, complete with carpet padding stapled to the walls, into a perfectly pink little girls' room, fit for Kennedy and Shelby.

We welcomed the challenge.

Orange paint, ripped-up flooring, and carpet-padded walls couldn't diminish the sense of pride we felt the day we closed on the house. CR and I did our final walk-through, and we found ourselves laughing in disbelief. This house was huge, too much house, if we were being honest, for a humble family of four. The home had three floors and five bedrooms and was over 3,500 square feet. As we made our way up to the third floor, I jokingly told CR, "I guess we're just going to have to fill this house with children." I certainly had no idea how true that statement would turn out to be.

Weeks passed as we got settled into our new home, and in the back of my mind I could feel the anticipation brewing. I knew that once I had checked off that final box, the "happy life" checklist was complete:

Marriage. *Check.*

Two kids. *Check.*

Good job. *Check.*

Homeownership. *Check.*

I was just waiting, rather impatiently, for the promised feeling to come, the one that held everything I'd ever hoped for, worked for, and dreamed of.

Contentment.

I had done everything right. I had married an amazing man, we had two healthy and happy kids, CR worked at the bank by day and coached baseball in the evenings, and now we finally owned a home.

Days turned to weeks and weeks turned to months, as I waited to feel what had been promised to me all my life. Every choice I'd made up until now was intended to bring me one step closer to this euphoria. I'd placed the final puzzle piece, I was ready to reap the reward of my perfectly executed plan. I was like an Olympic ice-skater who'd hit every triple loop, double salchow, and triple lutz to perfection. I was standing on the ice, head held high, heart pounding, hands thrown into the air waiting to hear the roar of applause.

But the feeling never came. That dull ache of discontent still lingered. I felt that I was doing all the things I'd been taught to do, and I didn't understand why I was still feeling this way.

I began to question whether perhaps the problem wasn't a faulty plan or an empty promise. Perhaps it was *me.*

Was I ungrateful? Did I not see my family, my home, my security as blessings from God? Was I somehow making God angry at for me for questioning it all? On the outside, everything seemed so perfect. I held it together, so no one knew the battle that was raging inside of me. The expectations came from my church, my friends, what I saw on TV and social media, and I'd internalized them as truths for myself:

You have to look cute and trendy but not so much that it appears you're trying too hard. You have to be sexy for your husband so he won't look elsewhere, but not so sexy that other men notice you—goodness, girl, you could cause them to stray! Speak kindly and gently to your kids, but don't be a pushover. Eat healthy and work out—you can't look like you just had a baby, you've got to snap back! Oh, but don't get too into fitness or your muscles might make you look manly. Besides, you can't let your own vanity and time at the gym keep you from spending every waking second with your precious babies. But don't give them so much attention that they think the world revolves around them. A good mom devotes herself fully to her kids and husband. Oh, but make sure you're filling your cup. . . . You can't pour from an empty cup!

Listening to these voices was utterly exhausting. I was drained and wanted to scream at the top of my lungs: "This *can't* be what we are made for!" I was playing a game so many of us play, and none of us will ever be able to win. The comparison game has no finish line, and only leaves us feeling depleted, exhausted, and desperate. It's not just a high bar to reach for—it's a totally unattainable one.

On Easter Sunday in 2011 I got the girls all dressed up and off to church we went. We had plans to do all the things: dye eggs, hunt Easter eggs, enjoy a meal with my family later. But as I sat watching a video in which the narrator spoke of the pain Jesus endured and what His last day on earth was really like, something started stirring deep within me.

I looked around at the hundreds of people, dressed to the nines on Easter Sunday, I thought of the parking lot full of minivans and SUVs, the comfortable homes we'd all go home to that day, the feasts most of us would eat. I pictured the eggs we would dye, the candy our kids would overeat that day, and the typical "dream" of a life most of us would return to after this service. The tears felt hot as they dripped down my face. Was this, this all-American, white-picket-fence, safe-on-the-sidelines life, what Jesus really died for? The shoe didn't quite seem to fit. How come some of us would have this life, while others born on the very same planet, loved by the very same God, wouldn't even have a chance at this life? How could this be God's plan for a fulfilled life if it wasn't available for everyone?

Praying, I cried out to Him, "Lord, break my heart for what breaks Yours. Give me eyes to see the world as You do. Help me to find the meaning and the purpose in this life. I love my life and I am so grateful, but I know You have more for me. I know there *must* be more than this dream I've been sold!"

I didn't get an immediate, lightning-bolt answer. But suddenly I had fresh eyes to see the world and a clearer mind to understand His words in a deeper and more honest way. I knew there was more, and I was determined to find it.

6

Kol Demama Daka

THE STILL, SMALL VOICE

Listen in silence because if your heart is full of other things you cannot hear the voice of God.

—Mother Teresa

As God opened my eyes to see the world as He does and opened my heart to explore this perspective further, I remembered the story in 1 Kings about Elijah. In the story, Elijah, after he defeats the prophets of Baal, seeks rest and some time with the Lord. He is feeling lost and alone, and he needs to hear from God. The Lord sends Elijah to the mountain to stand in His presence. The story then goes on to say a great and strong wind tore through the mountains, but the Lord was not in the wind. An earthquake came, but the Lord was not in the earthquake. A fire burned across the land, but the Lord was not in the fire.

But after the fire a gentle whisper followed. The Lord came to Elijah in that whisper: *kol demama daka*. Translated, the phrase means "the sound of thin silence." It's the kind of voice you can only hear when you quiet the world around you enough to hear it. You have to be listening for it.

I'd heard this story a handful of times growing up, but it wasn't until adulthood that its true meaning would become clear to me. That is how I've found I can hear God most clearly. When I stop brushing everything off as just a coincidence and start paying attention to the small signs He gives me. Sometimes it comes in the form of a number or dates. Other times, it's a feeling. The only way I know to describe the feeling is to imagine you are in the place that makes you feel the happiest in all the world, you're with the person or people you love most, your belly is full of delicious food, and you're at complete peace. That feeling, in that moment, is the same one that comes over me when I know God is the one leading me in a certain direction. For me, it's a feeling of belonging, like I know somehow that I fit in this particular story. Even if I don't know how or why,

I just fit. I belong in it; even if it's uncomfortable or not what I had envisioned, I still know I belong there.

I can come up with a lot of harebrained schemes, plans, and grand adventures. It can be hard to know which string to pull, which path to take, or which hill to die on that day. But it's that feeling of belonging that lets me know that God has placed me here. He wants me to keep going. More important, the feeling of belonging lets me know that the feelings I have are from Him. It's assurance that I'm where I need to be. If I can quiet the world around me, with its voices telling me who I should be, what I should look like, how many kids I should have, and even how I should worship God—when I can silence those voices, I can hear Him in the *kol demama daka*.

There is a second piece to hearing the Lord that I feel is equally important; that is, God doesn't contradict Himself. Throughout history, people have used "hearing from God" as a justification to forward their hateful, corrupt agendas. That's why it's important that whenever I feel God leading me toward something, one of my first moves is to read what His word has to say. Does what I feel He is asking me to do contradict His written word? If the answer is yes, then I know it's my own selfish desires and not a true calling He has placed on my heart. I'm not an expert on Scripture. I don't have the whole Bible memorized, and I'm not a theologian, but I don't believe God expects me to be. I believe He asks me to do the best with what knowledge and wisdom He has given me, and with the way I feel His presence guiding me in my prayer life. Ultimately, He wants me to continue to seek Him and His word, and to seek truth in the noise of this world.

It's easy to get wrapped up in what *we* want, especially because our culture tells us that we should always be happy, that we're in charge of our own happiness, and that we hold the key to it. If we aren't happy, the solution is simple: we just need to make the necessary changes to get happy. If only life were that easy. Perhaps this is the reason so many people choose to see their wants and desires as the highest priority. When we see people making decisions that seem contradictory to their own happiness and perceived safety, we question them and even grow concerned, instead of cheering them on and backing them up.

My personal struggle in adulthood has all too often been not a struggle to hear the voice of the Lord in my life, but a struggle to actually do what I feel He's asking of me. That's where I find my faith tested the most. Am I willing to not just be a hearer of the word, but a doer?

I wouldn't have to wait long to put my faith to the test. Big changes were stirring in my heart, and even bigger changes were coming down the road for our family.

7

Moved to Action

He is longing for an advocate to stand up and say,
"I am willing, God, to fight for what is Yours . . .
I am willing, God, burden me."

—Eric Ludy

I had been interested in adoption since I was a teenager, but one morning, a few weeks after my Easter service meltdown, I was reading my Bible when I came across the verse James 1:27: "Religion that God our Father accepts as pure and faultless is this: to look after orphans and widows in their distress and to keep oneself from being polluted by the world."

Those words pricked my heart.

Religion that God sees as *pure* is to look after the orphans and widows. My mind flashed back to that documentary about adoption I'd seen all those years ago in high school, and I thought of all the children who would fall asleep that night without a mother to kiss them goodnight.

Now that I was a mother myself, the sting of that pain felt real to me in a way it never had before. I thought of my own girls. What if that were my Kennedy? Alone, hungry, crying herself to sleep or, even worse, not crying at all because she'd already learned no one cared. No one would come to comfort her. What if Shelby slept on the floor with a hundred other children, with no blanket, no pillow?

I glanced up from my Bible to see my two girls giggling and dancing along to some silly song from *Barney and Friends*. They'd never known hunger or what it felt like to need me and not have me show up. All they knew was love and safety.

I swallowed hard to push down the lump in my throat, my nose stinging in anticipation of the waterworks building behind my eyes. I felt broken as I never had before. It was almost as if a blindfold had been removed, but it was one I never knew I had on to begin with. My hand swiftly went to my chest; I was surprised to find this pain had become a physical ache in my heart. Something different was happening, something I didn't see coming at all.

A feeling began to come over me, the same feeling I had felt when I decided to marry CR, when we had our sweet girls, and when we bought this house. A feeling of knowing I belonged in this story, there was a place for me here in this world of adoption. God was revealing His heart to me if I was ready to listen. I sat there on my couch feeling so many things that seemed contradictory, but they were existing together, at the same time: Brokenness and belonging. Heartbreak and hope. Faith and fear.

I began scouring the internet for information on adoption, staying up until the wee hours of the morning, filling spiral notebooks with pages of feverishly scratched-out notes. If I was going to seriously present this to CR, I knew I needed a lot more than a "feeling" to share with him.

The deeper I dived into this research, the more certain I became that this journey was exactly what the Lord had for us next, and the more questions about my faith started bubbling up. How in the sweet name of baby Jesus had I attended church almost all of my life and was only now hearing these truths? Why weren't all pastors everywhere calling on their congregations to move, to act, to do something—*anything*? It's such a complex issue, I understand; but why weren't churches running to these children, swimming across oceans, tearing down walls to help them? Why were we Christians doing practically nothing to help? Of course, I know now that there are so many who are taking action and living out what they believe, but the orphan crisis and all the complex issues surrounding it were never topics I heard preached about in church. I wanted to know why. I wanted to know how I'd sat through thousands of church services and had no idea that there are more than 430,000 children in foster care in the United States alone, and millions of children worldwide who need someone to fight for them.

In my research, I stumbled across a video by Eric Ludy called *Depraved Indifference*. In it, he explained how our world values fame, money, and talent, but the Kingdom of God is the exact opposite. God tells us that the prized ones are the weak ones—the ones who don't have someone to feed them, someone to protect them—these are the ones who should be treated as royalty here on earth. Ludy's words pelted my heart as if he were speaking a language I'd never heard but completely understood.

" 'The way you treat them is ultimately the way you're treating me.' What you do unto the least of these is how you're ultimately treating your God," Ludy declared.

I'd heard thousands of sermons, but never once had anyone so clearly and simply explained what God wanted from me, what it looked like to follow Him. No frills or big to-do, no flashy light show or high-production video—the message was uncomplicated and straightforward.

God is not here walking around on this earth, except through us.

Our hands are *His hands*, our feet are *His feet*, our heart is *His heart* here on earth.

He's a father to the fatherless, *through us*.

He restores the weak and the oppressed, *through us*.

I had to ask myself: Was I willing to leave my life of comfort and security to run recklessly toward the broken people in this hurting world? Would I choose to step into hard places and sit with those who are suffering, for the glory of our King? I'd become so distracted, believing that if I could just fill my life up with busyness, tasks, checklists, and to-do lists, my life would have purpose. I figured there were other people who were far better equipped to do the hard work and that maybe if I just ignored the impossibly heartbreaking truths, they would just go away.

The veil wasn't just being lifted—it was being ripped right off. I'd spent so many years crafting my life to fit perfectly into what others wanted from me and now the haze was dissipating. The questions I'd stuffed away while I was busy making everyone else happy were finally being answered. The measuring stick I'd used to determine the successes or failures in my life wasn't at all the one God used. Pleasing God and finding purpose were far simpler endeavors than I'd made them for the past twenty-seven years.

The next step was to talk to CR about what I felt God was calling our family to. Adoption had been something CR and I discussed very early on in our marriage, so I knew he wasn't going to flat-out say no, but it had been years since I'd uttered a word about the topic. We weren't exactly rolling in money at this point in our lives. CR was working two jobs, I had just started a photography business and was still in the process of getting it off the ground, and we had two young daughters whom we had decided to homeschool. Life was full, and we had enough money to get by but not much extra. I really expected him to brush me off or at least tell me we had to wait a few years—as we moms tell our kids who are pleading for something to "ask me later," hoping they'll forget about it altogether. Yeah, that's the kind of brush-off I was expecting to get.

A few nights after feverishly doing my research, I approached CR and poured my heart out. I told him about the epiphany I'd had and the way I felt God was speaking to me. I cried as I shared the video I'd found online and told CR how I couldn't stand the thought of our girls needing someone to stand in the gap for them and having no one show up. My voice was shaky but certain.

Even through my emotional meltdown, CR could hear what my heart was trying to say. And much to my surprise, he was open to it. He wanted some time to pray about it on his own, but we both knew there wasn't much left to wrestle with. This was the door God was asking us to walk through. On the other side was complete uncertainty, but we took each other's hands and walked through the door together.

8

Written in the Sand

Faith is taking the first step, even when
you don't see the whole staircase.

—Martin Luther King Jr.

In July 2011, I was hearing God more clearly than I ever had in my life—not in the booming voice of Morgan Freeman or anything, but in a quiet and assuring way. A gentle nudge, like a hand on my lower back, leading me to the next right decision. That still, small voice. After much prayer and discussion, CR and I decided we would adopt a girl, and

I spent countless hours praying for her. Was she born yet? What was her story? What did she look like?

My thoughts of her would keep me up at night. I thought about what she would look like, her hair color, her eyes; every little detail of her my imagination would piece together. One evening, as I lay in bed envisioning her, I felt God was whispering her name to me: *Rose.* I smiled. I knew who God intended her to be, and it was now just a matter of when I would meet her. I felt so strongly that this was the name we would give our sweet baby girl.

A few months later, the leaves turned to brilliant fall colors, the air became crisp, and we decided to take a weekend trip to the beach. CR and I both had been working so hard, and with our jobs, adoption paperwork, raising money to adopt, and parenting two vivacious little girls, we needed the downtime.

CR spent most of the trip splashing around in the indoor pool with the girls, and I stayed curled up in a beach chair reading books about adoption. There was so much I didn't know, and I was hungry to read real-life stories and to find others who felt the same way I did. I read one memoir in particular that struck a chord within me. The story was about a young girl who'd left her whole life behind to follow Jesus into the unknown. I never really knew anyone who'd been so bold, and I was inspired by her story.

This was the kind of life I wanted. I didn't know it until this moment, but something about her story was igniting a passion within me that had been lying dormant. My life had always been about making other people happy and trying to maintain the status quo. God was opening my eyes to a life that looked different, perhaps even weird, but something about it all just felt right. Now I was seeing what could be possible, what it could look like to have the kind of life that didn't allow fear to be in the driver's seat, the kind of life that walked the walk rather than just talking the talk. This was my peek into what it might be like to lay down the dreams I'd been sold, for the chance to follow Jesus and perhaps find the life I'd been missing all this time.

If I could just quiet the noise of the world and lean in close to the voice of my heavenly Father, if I could just keep my eyes fixed on Him, I knew my life could have the depth and the meaning I'd craved for so long. I'd been given a purpose that was so much greater than myself. I felt that— much as trainers place blinders on racehorses so they won't see and be distracted by the horses running alongside them but just focus on their race—God was placing blinders on my mind's eye, giving me full permission to ignore what other people were doing, what direction the herd was going in. He wanted me to focus on my own race, the one He had set before me, to keep my eyes focused on Him, waiting for me at the finish line.

As the sun set on that day, we set out for a family walk on the beach. It was quiet; the wind was just a whisper. Maybe it was the words I'd read earlier, which were like musical notes floating around in my mind, or maybe it was the power of the ocean or the beauty of the sunset—whatever the reason,

I felt closer to God and His plan for my life than I ever had before. I was certain of His voice and of what He had told me a few months earlier about our future daughter.

I reached down, grabbed a twig, and began to scratch into the sand the letters R-O-S-E.

She was out there, my Rose, just waiting for me.

9

This Is Africa

I have found the paradox, that if you love until it hurts,
there can be no more hurt, only more love.

—Mother Teresa

Our decision to adopt was met with mixed responses. Many
people were excited for us, some were cautiously happy,
and others were flat-out disapproving. I was still in the early
stages of being a recovering people-pleaser, which made
every snarky remark, discouraging email, and sideways
glance hard for me to shake.

But God had presented an open door, and we were carefully and timidly stepping through it. We started working
on our home study, since we knew that would be a require-
ment no matter where we chose to adopt from. I turned to

Google once more, and after reading review after review, eventually landed on a small but well-loved home study agency. Our social worker was eager to help us get started, and within a few weeks we had our first mountain of paperwork to climb. Background checks, financial statements, medical records, and more were required to qualify us for an adoption.

With this part of the process under way, the next step was to choose the place from which we would adopt. I knew people who had adopted from Ethiopia, Uganda, and China. We initially thought we'd do a domestic infant adoption, but, truthfully, the idea of having an open adoption, with the possibility of another mother in my child's life, scared me to death. I didn't think I could handle that. We began researching all the options and, more important, where we actually qualified to adopt from. China had been in my heart since high school, but that option was off the table: we were barely twenty-seven years old, and China requires you to be thirty years old to adopt.

We decided to start the process in Ethiopia, however, that plan was quickly thwarted when the adoption process in the country was changed and it looked like adoptions were coming to a screeching halt. In my research I stumbled upon a small pilot program in the Congo that was just getting started and we seemed to meet all the requirements.

Can I be honest? I knew little to nothing about the Democratic Republic of the Congo (DRC) when we began this journey. But now that my work researching adoption had made me into something like a private investigator, I began digging and absorbing all the information I could. I found dozens of documentaries, books, and articles about the DRC and its history. What I uncovered was not only shocking; it was heartbreaking. The DRC was known as the most unstable country in Africa, and a senior United Nations official even called it the "rape capital of the world."* Let that sink in. This country is one of the richest in the world, with natural resources such as diamonds, gold, copper, coltan, and even timber and oil found there. Because of its immense economic value, the country has been in a state of war for decades, with rebels using sexual violence as means to control the people, keeping them in fear.

Yet even through all this pain, the resilience and the bravery of the people were what struck me the most. Despite all the foreigners who had come from all over the world to steal and control the riches of the earth there, the people fought back. They had pride in their heritage, and they seem to never lose the hope of someday regaining what continues to be stolen from them. I began to fall in love with the Congolese people, their rich history and traditions, their fortitude and determination. They were

*"Tackling sexual violence must include prevention, ending impunity—UN official," *UN News*, April 27, 2010, https://news.un.org/en/story/2010/04/336662.

inspiring to me. I knew this was the right place for us to begin our adoption journey.

We had been on the list waiting for a little girl since I knew so clearly that God had told me I had a daughter named Rose. After months of waiting, I received a call from our agency caseworker. She said, "I know you're on the list for a girl, but we have this baby boy; he's only two months old. The other families ahead of you have all said no; they want to wait for a girl. Are you interested?"

There was zero hesitation. I just blurted out, "Of course we are, yes . . . yes . . . yes . . . we want him!"

I hung up the phone and dropped to my knees in prayer. I told God maybe I had misunderstood. I didn't know why God had told me the name "Rose"—maybe I was wrong? Maybe I had misheard Him? I didn't have the answer, but I did know without a shadow of a doubt that we were supposed to say yes to this baby boy.

CR agreed without any hesitation as well. I was nervous about how he'd react, seeing as how I'd told the agency yes without asking him first, but seeing his excitement assured me that this was the right choice. Sometimes the path changes; the road shifts in a direction you don't see coming. While I'm almost always up for a pivot, CR likes to be steadfast, to stay the course. It's an admirable quality, but we quickly learned that in adoption, you need to be ready to be flexible, to do the unexpected. There's almost nothing straightforward or predictable in this process. I was thankful CR saw this the same way I did, and we hit the ground running, ready to get our son home.

The day it finally happened, the day I got the official referral call, I called CR and asked him to come home early. The email with the little boy's medical file and photo sat in my inbox while I paced the front walk impatiently waiting for CR to arrive. I wanted us to be together when we saw our son for the first time. CR came peeling into the driveway, and before he could even put his bag down I'd begun pulling up the message. We glanced over his file, but to be honest, I could not have cared less what his medical conditions were; nothing would have changed my mind. I opened the file for the photo, and there he was, with big brown eyes (one that was drooping closed a bit), a little blue onesie, and barely any hair. He was perfect, he was our son: Noah.

When we began the adoption process with the DRC, I knew that it was a pilot program for our agency. Agency workers were new to Congolese adoptions, and I tried to be patient as they worked out the details of each step in the process. We hit a point at the very end of the process when my mama instincts kicked in and I just knew I needed to go there and make sure things were being completed in a timely and ethical manner. As I mentioned previously, I'm relentless when it comes to something I care about—but when it's about my child? I become unstoppable.

I'd made friends with a number of adoptive parents who'd completed Congolese adoptions recently, and they gave me all kinds of sage advice, but the most valuable was that to get things done in a timely fashion, I needed to be in country. Noah's adoption was complete; we were waiting on the little details like his passport and exit letter. I knew what I had to do.

Kennedy and Shelby were six and four at the time, and we knew that if both CR and I left them for an unknown amount of time it could be very hard and perhaps even damaging for them. As important as getting Noah home was, I also wanted to make sure my sweet girls were taken care of during this important time of change in our family. Since CR had a job that didn't allow him to just up and move to Africa for an undisclosed amount of time, we decided he would stay home with the girls. I still wanted someone to travel with me, so my mom volunteered to go. My mom loves to travel and meet new people, and she's sensible, quick on her feet, and fierce as a lion when she needs to be. I knew she was the perfect person to accompany me on this journey.

I called my agency and told them I'd purchased plane tickets and was coming to get my son. As you can imagine, they were not thrilled that I was taking matters into my own hands, but they agreed to help me once I arrived in country.

I'll never forget the drive from the airport to our lodging place, a Catholic procure nestled in the heart of Kinshasa. These drivers put NASCAR drivers to shame—bobbing and weaving, flying through red lights, barely missing pedestrians. It was terrifying and amazing all at the same time.

Once we arrived at our lodging, Mom and I dropped our bags onto the queen-size bed we were sharing and just looked at each other with relief. Not only did we survive the car ride over, but we were finally here, mere miles away from Noah. I had watched him grow for months from thousands of miles away, praying that he was safe, that he wasn't hungry or alone, and that someone was taking care of him. He was nine months old now, and it was finally time to meet him and bring him home to his new family.

Mom and I woke early the next morning, anxious to greet the day. This was going to be a day to remember, the day I took my son out of the orphanage and into our family. As we sipped our coffee and I nibbled my toast, too nervous to eat much else, I just praised God over and over in my head.

"Thank You, God, for including me in Your story for Noah. I'm so grateful to be a part of it. You didn't have to write me in, and yet, You have. Thank You."

We greeted our attorney in the lobby, and he let me know very matter-of-factly that while I could go to the orphanage and meet Noah today, I was not allowed to take him home yet. The attorney informed us that there was a piece of paper that needed a signature, and until we had it, Noah couldn't leave.

I was so upset! I'd never heard of this document before, and I feared this was just a way to put me in my place since I had come without permission. None of that mattered, though; there was nothing I could do. So I tried my best to focus on the joy of the day. I was meeting Noah. I might not be taking him with me that day, but at least I was finally going to lay eyes on him and hold him in my arms. I'd waited so long but that would have to be enough for today.

When we arrived at the gates of the orphanage I found it to be far worse than I'd even expected. There were broken boards with protruding nails all over the dirty, urine-soaked floor. The smells are what still stick with me to this day. If despair had a smell, this was it. I'd been warned that he was in one of the worst orphanages in the city, but this was beyond anything I could have imagined. We made our way through the small entry and I had the distinct feeling that I was being watched.

I glanced to my right through a window fitted with metal bars, like a prison. Behind the bars were hundreds of eyes peering at me. I'd barely entered the main living area when a woman holding a baby greeted me. He turned to look at me, and I knew right away that it was my Noah. I gently plucked him from her arms as the tears welled in my eyes. All I wanted to do in that moment was run—to get him the hell out of there. These were not conditions for children; they weren't even fit for a dog. I could hardly believe what I was seeing.

The woman guided us over to the one sofa that sat in the

corner of an empty, concrete room. I sat down and tried to just soak in Noah, his face, his hands, his little lips. But all I could see were the kids who began to fill the room, almost totally silent, watching us. My gaze would meet theirs, and without a word being said, I knew what they were thinking: "Why not me? Will anyone ever come for me?"

If I had thought God cracked my heart wide open before, He had all but shattered it now. These kids had zero toys, no chairs to sit in, no shoes, barely any food, and no mama. I continued my futile attempt to connect with Noah, despite the desperation that filled the air. I don't know how long I was there, what I said to anyone, or even what color the couch was. There were more than a hundred children there that day, but I remember almost every detail of their faces, especially their eyes—I'll never forget the sadness in their eyes. To this day, Mom and I cannot speak of that day in Kinshasa without getting emotional. It changed us both in ways we didn't fully understand until after we had returned home.

Three days later, we finally got the call that the elusive paper had been signed, although no one was ever able to show it to me, and I'm still not sure it ever actually existed. My frustration was washed away as I learned that Noah was finally going to be brought to me.

That night, I fumbled around the halls of the procure,

which suddenly seemed like a maze as I made my way down to the lobby. I flung the door open, and there he was, sound asleep on the shoulder of our caseworker. She said, "He cried himself to sleep on the way over. The orphanage said he's been crying ever since you left."

I lifted his limp body from her arms, and he continued to sleep. I stroked his back and just breathed him in while we talked. Once the logistical things were done, we headed back up to our room. He was beginning to wake. I didn't know how he'd respond when he opened his eyes and found himself in a new place, with this highly emotional white lady, but as he cracked his eyes open, a smile spread across his little face. He seemed happy to see me. I knew there would be grieving and heartbreak to come, but for the time being, he seemed to be handling the transition well.

We played a little and I attempted to feed him, although he didn't seem too interested. I'm sure his little nerves had his tummy in an upheaval too. Mom and I took countless photos of him, and I called home to let CR know that I finally had our son! I could hear them all screaming through the phone with joy and excitement. Even though this wasn't your typical event of meeting the baby at the hospital and taking five hundred photos, it was so beautiful in its own way.

I suddenly had an intense urge to give Noah a bath. He seemed settled enough that it wouldn't terrify him, so I grabbed our little shower bucket and began to fill it with warm water from the hot pot. There was no hot water at our procure, so we had to improvise to avoid a freezing cold shower.

I gently submerged his little body in the water, and it was clear he'd never had a real bath before. I could sense Noah's hesitation as his little muscles tightened up, but he relaxed quickly. I lathered up his body and I could feel the tears swelling in my eyes. With every pour of water I was washing away more than just dirt. This bath was a cleansing, a renewal. He was always valuable, always a beloved child of God, but now his previous status of "orphan" was being washed away. He was now my beloved son. I was struck by how this was the most accurate picture of the gospel I'd ever seen. God rescues us from our former lives, pulls us in close, and cleanses us of our past transgressions, and we emerge as his beloved sons and daughters. But God wasn't using me to rescue Noah; God was rescuing *me*. From this point forward my life would be split in half: before Africa, and after. I'd never be the same woman again.

As I lay in bed that night and cuddled with Noah, I felt the heavy weight that this was a baby who never should have been mine. As grateful as I was to have this chance to be his mama, it was only possible because another woman lost her son. My heart ached for her. It also ached for Noah, whom I would bring to a home with safety, love, and a wealth of resources, but who would lose things too. He was losing the opportunity to grow up in his own culture, in his country, with his birth parents. I'd always heard that adoption is born from loss, and until that moment, I don't think I fully understood the significance of those words.

As the thrill of the newness of it all began to wear off, Noah's little heart began to mourn. I slipped him into the baby carrier close to my body, and we paced the halls of the procure, mourning together. He was only nine months old, and it seemed he was losing everything. I was twenty-eight years old and losing the innocence I'd been blinded by most of my life. This story of adoption God called me into was proving to be far messier than I'd ever imagined.

10

Fight, Flight, Freeze

God whispers to us in our pleasures, speaks
in our conscience, but shouts in our pain: it is
His megaphone to rouse a deaf world.

—C. S. Lewis

We'd spent the day at a small orphanage just outside
Kinshasa. I had already been on the verge of falling in love
with the Congolese people, but my time spent with the
orphanage nannies and babies that day turned my budding
romance into a full-blown love affair. I'd witnessed the re-
siliency of these women who dedicated their lives to caring
for children who, through no fault of their own, had found

themselves abandoned on the streets. I watched as the nannies lovingly prepared their meals, danced with them, and scooped them up to comfort them when their wild dancing earned them a skinned knee. The nannies loved all these children as their own.

When the day was nearing its end, we loaded up and began the hour-long drive back to the procure. It had been a long and emotionally exhausting day, the roads were bumpy, and the tropical humidity had me dripping with sweat. I snuggled Noah in my lap, gently running my fingers through the small patch of curly hair atop his head. I prayed over him and his birth country that had now become so very precious to me. My mind was in another place, until I realized the usual hum of the people hurrying through the streets had quieted, and the voices of men singing in unison had risen above the street noise.

I was sitting in the back seat behind the passenger's side, so I leaned over to see what was ahead of us. It was a military tanker overflowing with soldiers who were singing and using their assault rifles like drumsticks against the sides of the tank.

My heart began to race.

From my encounters with the military in the United States, I was used to the presence of the military bringing a sense of safety. This encounter felt like exactly the opposite.

Our driver was a Congolese man in his fifties who had such a joyful spirit about him. Earlier, at the orphanage, I'd watched him pick up the tiniest three-year-old girl I'd ever seen and swing her around while she giggled. He looked at her with such love it made my heart want to burst. But now a look of concern swept across his face.

I'd hoped to see him roll his eyes, as if to say, "Oh, boy, here these goofballs go again," but that was clearly *not* his sentiment.

The soldiers had begun to climb out of the tank, and it was then I noticed the women. Wearing not much, they climbed on top of the tank and started dancing. They didn't look excited to be there.

My uneasiness grew into panic, my heart racing as the soldiers made their way through the streets that had now become a parking lot. I tried to take a few deep breaths while the voices in my head started a desperate and futile attempt at calming me down. I looked over at Mom and her expression only affirmed my feeling that we were possibly in serious danger here.

Furious thoughts ran through my head: "They won't hurt you, you're an American." "God wouldn't bring you all the way across the world to adopt this baby just to have you die in the Congo."

Logically, these thoughts all made sense.

But when the people who had been frozen like statues on the streets began to flee down alleys, climb fences, and jump off the small cliff just to the right of our car, I knew these soldiers were not the kind I could trust.

Fear took over my body, and the urge to run came over

me, too. The slow-motion feeling of all that was happening around me was quickly thrust into real time when Noah began to cry. He'd been asleep on my lap this whole time, and now here I was, this twenty-eight-year-old American woman, holding a crying Congolese baby boy on my lap.

I immediately felt like a target.

I did the only thing I could think to do. I slipped him down my shins and tried to tuck him under the seat in front of me.

The sound of the soldiers' singing grew louder as they inched closer to our car. I was slouched so far down in my seat, desperately trying to conceal Noah from their sight. I watched through a sliver of space between the passenger's headrest and window as the soldiers began ripping people out of their cars and off the bus. They were indiscriminately punching people and kicking them, and I'm pretty sure my heart stopped completely as one soldier pulled his gun and pointed it at a man cowering on the ground. I truly believed that in that moment I was going to witness a man be slaughtered on the street. I began to pray harder than I ever had in my life for the Lord to protect our car and to protect that man. We were mere feet away, and I knew that God was the only one who could prevent us from becoming the next victims. It felt like a nightmare; but this wasn't a nightmare, it was real. There was no waking up in the safety of my bed. I could only pray with every fiber of my being for the Lord to intervene, and so I did.

I later learned that this was the way the military and

police controlled the Congolese people, with fear and intimidation. With their singing and casual attitude, it seemed as though to them this was just a fun game, a way to kill time. Thankfully, the soldier did not pull the trigger on that man that day, and with immense relief I watched as they turned in the opposite direction from us, climbed back onto the tank, and rode away laughing and singing. That was the scariest moment of my life, but all I could think of on the somber drive back to the procure was that, for the Congolese people, this was their everyday life. There was no escape from the terror. I was thankful for the freedom I experience every day, while also heartbroken that the friends I was making here in the DRC did not have that same freedom and safety.

I was stunned by the kindness and joy we found as we got to know the Congolese people, despite the terrors and lack of resources that they lived with on a daily basis. Over the course of the month we spent in Kinshasa, my mom and I watched a good number of other adoptive families come and go. The staff treated each and every one of them with so much love and tender care, I found myself at times being envious of the staff members' inherent joyfulness. They didn't have much by our American standards to be happy about. They were barely scraping by, their country was struggling, and they had little to no protection and not much hope things would change anytime soon. And yet, they were joyful.

Most of the people we encountered there were believers,

and it was as if I had met a whole new breed of Christian: people who loved the Lord and trusted Him and His goodness despite their circumstances. These people were showing me what it meant to have the true "joy of the Lord." Moreover, they were opening my eyes to how one-sided my view of Christianity had been. I didn't realize until this trip how Americanized my view of Jesus was. I'd been raised with the idea that when the Lord showed favor, it looked like being flooded with earthly blessings, safety, and a risk-free life. Somewhere along the way, the American dream had become synonymous with God's design for our life, and I was seeing with my own eyes that this couldn't be further from the truth. Little by little I was learning what loving Him and trusting Him really looked like. The Congolese people I'd been getting to know had a bold and authentic faith that made mine seem tame and colorless. Even though my mind was necessarily preoccupied with Noah, adoption paperwork, and visas, it was clear to me that I still had a lot to learn about what it looked like to follow Jesus.

Thanks to technology, I am actually able to keep in touch with a few of the people we befriended while we were in the DRC. They are able to see Noah grow up, and I am counting down the days until Noah is old enough that we can bring him back to the DRC and allow him to experience the beauty of his country and heritage firsthand.

11

Everything Changed

ONE WORLD, TWO TRUTHS

God's definition of what matters is pretty straightforward.
He measures our lives by how we love.

—Francis Chan

I slipped off my clothes and, for the first time in six weeks, stepped into a hot shower. The steam rose up, I closed my eyes, and my mind drifted right back to the DRC. Just twenty-four hours before, I'd been warming water in a hot pot and taking baths in a bucket meant to wash dishes in.

I knew reentry would be hard, but I couldn't just forget everything I'd seen during my time in Africa. I'm not sure what I had expected to happen when I got home. Had I expected that I'd come back and just pick back up my normal life again? I guess in some ways, I naively had. I didn't know what I was walking into when I arrived in the DRC, and I had no idea how immensely hard it would be to walk away. After our terrifying encounter with the Congolese military, my last days there had been filled with such desperation to get out and get Noah safely home that I didn't really prepare my heart to be back in the land of plenty and abundance.

Everywhere I went, I could see the faces of the children at the orphanage. If I felt hungry, I could just head to the pantry to grab a snack; no need to worry that the food wouldn't be there or that there wouldn't be enough for all my children to eat that day. In fact, there was far more than enough. Now when I slid open the pantry door, instead of seeing all the boxes of cereal and crackers, I'd see the face of a little boy I'd encountered.

I remembered that we had been in the DRC only for a day or two when our driver took us out to run some adoption paperwork errands. We didn't have Noah yet at that time, and I was still taking everything in, trying to make sense of this entirely new world. We stopped at a traffic light; I looked out the window, and my eyes instantly met his. He looked to be about six years old, his clothes were tattered and filthy, and his shoes were so full of holes that all of his toes were sticking out. His eyes were the most beautiful shade of brown, and his lashes were full and long enough to make any woman envious.

No words were needed.

His hand gently reached up, and he placed his fingertips on the glass between us. I had no food with me, only money. Without hesitation I grabbed for my purse. Before I could pull my wallet from inside, our driver said sternly: "No, Mrs. Angela, you cannot give money to the street children. This will create a big problem. They will all come. You cannot."

I lowered my purse back down into my lap, and when I looked at the boy again, he began to rub his bulging, distended belly. I felt like my heart was being ripped out right there on the streets of Kinshasa. The boy was clearly starving, and, as much as it hurt me to admit, I knew our driver was right. There were a hundred more children just like him scouring this very street for a scrap to eat. The light turned and, as we drove away, I watched his frail body grow smaller with distance. I found myself feeling angry with God. I didn't know how to process what I had just seen. Even though I had seen people regularly begging on nearly every highway off-ramp in our American city, that was nothing like this.

This boy had a look of desperation, of hopelessness, that I'd never seen before this moment.

Back home, the boy's emaciated face haunted me nearly every time I opened my fridge. Our needs were not just met but exceeded. We had an abundance of food; heck, I even spent most of my life refusing to eat leftovers because they didn't taste as good as the first time around. I found myself passing harsh judgments, not just on myself, but on everyone around me, too.

I was spiraling out of control. I had no earthly clue how to make sense of these two worlds. How was it possible for them both to exist under the same sun, the same stars—the same God? How come my children had the audacity to turn their noses up at what I'd made for dinner, when that boy would have taken and happily eaten anything I could have given him? I felt like I'd been to another planet. My heart and mind continued to attempt to hold these two truths at the same time. The paradox sometimes felt crippling.

I felt that no one understood what I had seen. My mom was the only one who'd been there and seen it all, and I could see she was wrestling with the same emotions and questions as I was. CR was still living in the same blissful ignorance I previously had enjoyed, not knowing the harsh realities of life in developing nations. I had told him everything, and he was sympathetic and heartbroken by the stories, but he hadn't seen the reality with his own eyes; it wasn't branded onto his heart as it was on mine.

Another memory that I couldn't shake was when I took Noah for his first scheduled medical appointment at the local hospital in Kinshasa. It was just around the corner from our procure, so Mom and I decided we'd walk and meet our agency rep there. Leaving the procure was always scary for me; my pale skin and red hair made me stick out like a sore thumb, and when you add in the baby, who clearly wasn't my biological child, people stared pretty hard. I was a smidge paranoid and a little jumpy, too, so I was happy to find refuge indoors.

The hospital waiting room was so overflowing with people, it was standing room only. It seemed more like a busy DMV office than a sterile hospital.

Mom and I found a little corner to sit and wait for Noah's medical exam. I flopped down on the floor, tired both emotionally and physically. Noah had begun grieving, and that meant I spent most of the evening pacing the halls with a baby crying himself to sleep. It was heartbreaking to witness, and as much as I wanted him to love me the same way I did him, I knew his little heart needed time to grieve. It was time for Noah's bottle, so I unzipped my backpack and started mixing up his formula. I looked up and my eyes instantly met hers: a young mama sitting across the room, holding what appeared to be a baby in her arms. We exchanged knowing smiles, one mama to another. We were both hot and sweaty and had arms full of babies. There's a camaraderie there that crosses cultures and languages. A tired mama is a tired mama.

A moment later her little one moved, and the blanket fell enough to expose the child sleeping in her mother's arms. The mother wasn't holding a baby. Her child was likely three or four, and every single bone seemed to protrude from under her thin skin. She looked as though she was dying. I had no idea why or what was wrong. I didn't know what to say or what I could do. Our eyes met again but this time she lowered hers quickly as though she felt ashamed or embarrassed. Our agency rep grabbed my hand and swiftly pulled me up: "Let's go, they're calling us back now." I scrambled to gather our things and get Noah on my hip, all the while trying to keep one eye on this precious mama.

The entire time the doctors looked over Noah, all I could think of was her. Was her child sick? Starving? Did she just need some money? I didn't know what, if anything, I could do. When we came out of the appointment I looked for her, but she was gone. I don't know if she got any help. I don't know if her child was admitted to the hospital that day. I don't know whether her child survived.

The other children in Noah's orphanage, the little boy on the street, the woman in the hospital: they were just a few of the many faces that haunted me upon returning home to the well-resourced West. My mind was in a constant battle while, outwardly, on the home front, things appeared to be perfect.

Noah slipped right into our family as if he'd always been there. CR was beaming with pride now that he was a father to three kids. Having a son was something he had always hoped to experience, and neither one of us had known whether this day would ever come. Noah was a dream come true for us. His sisters, Kennedy and Shelby, couldn't keep their hands off him. They were always picking him up and dragging him all over the house as if he were their new baby doll. You might be tempted to feel sorry for Noah, but he loved every second of it. Our whole family was enamored with him! We would clap and sing little songs we made up for him, and Noah would dance and bounce around with as much glee as I've seen in a child.

Nothing is ever perfect of course. There were nights where I'd rock him as he cried uncontrollably and for what seemed like no reason at all. Looking back, I realize he was processing a lot in those early days: a broken heart, fear, and trauma. All these can imprint on a child's brain, whether adopted as an infant or a teenager. People often assume that if you adopt a child as an infant, somehow, the child will be able to bypass that feeling, but that's simply not true. Even the tiniest of babies will grieve. I did my best to give Noah all the time and space his little heart needed to work through it.

Soon enough the sleepless and tear-filled nights became distant memories, and we began to feel like a "normal" family again. All the while, my internal battle raged on. CR was desperate to understand what I was going through; he was there for me in any and every way he could possibly think of, but no amount of assurance or encouraging words could seem to quiet the storm that was brewing inside of me. Something had to give.

Noah had just turned one, and it was his first Christmas in our home. My mental tug-of-war was taking its toll, and so CR sent me to do one of the things I enjoy most: going

Christmas shopping. He insisted we needed some new decorations and sent me on my way.

It's no secret to my friends and family how much I love Christmas. I often start listening to Christmas music in the late fall. I'm *that* person—which explains why CR thought sending me out into the holiday hustle and bustle might lift my spirits a bit.

As I strolled the aisles of Hobby Lobby, my senses were filled with all the things I loved. The smell of evergreen, the sound of carols, the twinkling lights on the rows of perfectly flocked trees. I paused for a moment to take in a gorgeous manger scene that had been set up, and I couldn't help but wonder: Was all this extravagance bad? Was it just a waste of money? Would Jesus be angry if He saw the receipt at checkout knowing His children were starving?

I left without purchasing anything and just sat in my car. I knew what I needed to find. The *kol demama daka*, the thin silence. I knew He would meet me there. Over the past few months, I'd been angry with God in a way I'm not sure I fully recognized, so I'd avoided Him. I'd considered myself a woman of strong faith by this point in my life, but looking into the eyes of a starving child will challenge everything you think you believe. I'd begged God to break my heart for what broke His; I guess I should have been better prepared for what that might mean, but I wasn't. I didn't know that what He would reveal to me would end up being the thing that challenged what I believed about

God, too, and about His goodness. I'd like to give you the resolution to it all and tell you that somehow God wrapped this one up with a tidy little bow for me. But I can't. In fact, holding the paradox is an everyday struggle for me.

I've learned to hold the resources I've been given with an open hand, being willing to let them go if I feel God calling me to something else. I never want things to tie me down if I feel Him asking me to move out in faith. And I believe money is a tool, just like any other tool, that can be used to change people's lives and that God can use to move forward His Kingdom.

I can change the world for one child, one person, one day at a time. We all can. It's easy to think that because we can't fix all the world's problems, we just shouldn't even try. I'll admit, it's overwhelming. But we can do one small act—the next right thing. We can make one small sacrifice each day, and they will all add up. There are certainly big-picture issues, such as creating sustainability and using ethical practices, and reversing poverty is a complex issue, but the first step is in our hearts. When we open our hearts, we realize that it could have just as easily been you or me in any painful situation around the world. It could have been me holding a dying a baby in a hospital in Kinshasa; it could have been my daughter, at five years old, begging on the streets for food. It could have been any of us, in any of these scenarios. When I think about those kids being my kids, the narrative changes.

When you consider that we are to love our neighbor as ourselves, ask what you yourself would want to happen. We have to let that pain move through us, let it hurt us, let the emotions flow out of us. Then, we take all that and let it move us to action.

12

Difficult roads often lead to beautiful destinations.

—Zig Ziglar

"Did you know that lobsters don't actually mate for life?" I said to CR as I stared into the tank in the restaurant lobby. He chuckled and placed his hand softly on my back. I get so awkward when I'm nervous and tend to blurt out anything that comes into my head without filtering it first. I could tell he was thinking, "Just get it all out now. This woman is gonna think we're complete weirdos if you keep doing that."

It was March 2013, and our desire to expand our family once again had led us to adoption—domestic infant adoption to be exact. This time I thought we might end up adopting the baby girl I had felt God place in my heart two years ago. Noah had settled so perfectly into our family, and we knew we wanted to give him a sibling close in age, just as the girls had with each other. We'd seen how strong their bond was, and I knew from my own relationship with my sisters how special a sibling was. Noah was only a little more than a year old, but we also knew the process could take a very long time, so we decided to get the ball rolling sooner rather than later.

After a quick and relatively painless home study update, we built our family's profile book and began the "presentation phase." This is just fancy wording for showing your book to expectant mamas and waiting to be chosen by one of them to raise their baby. The process is as gut-wrenching as it sounds, on both sides. I think even the most confident people in the world would begin to crumble under the pressure and wonder why they weren't picked each time. Was it the way we looked? Our house? Something we had written in the letter? I remember the first rejection as clearly as if it were yesterday. Our home study and profile book had just been completed when we got a call about a baby in Florida. The parents were high-school students. They had made this decision together and were choosing the family together as well. They even had *their* parents' support. It was really a unique situation but a beautiful one full of love and understanding from all involved.

We were told not to get our hopes up, as the couple had many more families than expected send in books, and the odds weren't in our favor. A couple weeks went by, the due date was approaching, and the agency called to tell us the news. The young couple had narrowed it down to two families, and we were one of them. Apparently, the expectant mama liked one family, and the dad liked another. We were so hopeful and prayed that if this baby girl was meant to be ours, the Lord would make it abundantly clear to *both* the parents. The whole concept of this kind of adoption was still very abstract in my mind. This baby has so many people who loved her and wanted what was best for her. Her mom and dad were trying to make the life-altering decision of allowing her to be raised by someone else—a decision I'm not sure I'd ever be brave enough to make—yet, here they were, just babies themselves, walking this difficult road. I prayed for them daily, and then the call finally came. They'd chosen the other family.

It's hard to prepare yourself for all the noes you'll hear before you actually hear a yes in the adoption world. Truth be told, it's also easy to make it all about you—or at least for me it was. In hindsight, I spent far too much time thinking of myself in this process: about how much the noes hurt me or about why the parents didn't like us. We heard a handful more noes before the call came that changed our lives.

I was leaving an appointment when I saw that I had missed a call from our adoption attorney. We had placed our profile book with multiple agencies and private attorneys who facilitate adoptions. We had just become an "active profile" with this attorney the week before, so to see she was calling already caught me off guard. I allowed myself to get a little bit excited. I called her back immediately and got her voice mail. My heart was racing with anticipation. I had three little kids in the back seat who had no clue what was going on; they just wanted to get to the playdate I'd promised them. We made the quick drive over to my friend's house so the kids could play while she and I chatted—you know, a mommy playdate. My attempts at making small talk were pathetic. I clutched my phone and prayed it would ring. After a grueling fifteen minutes that felt like five hours, the phone rang! I sprung from my friend's couch as if my hair were on fire and ran upstairs where I could answer the call in private.

On the other end was our attorney, and she uttered the words I'd been so anxious to hear: "You've been chosen." The excitement I felt was just as it had been with my previous children. Whether it was a positive pregnancy test or a "chosen" call, these were sacred times for me. God was revealing His greatest blessing to me, and I just stood in awe, heart bursting with gratitude every time.

That euphoric feeling began to slowly melt away as the attorney revealed the details of this story, what this expectant mama had been through, and why she was choosing adoption. It was heartbreaking.

Elle, as I'll call her, was in her early twenties, and this was to be her fourth baby. After her third baby was born, she had asked to have her tubes tied but was denied because the hospital she delivered at was a Catholic hospital and didn't offer any sterilization procedures. Elle worked three jobs to try to keep food on the table and was desperate to change her life. When she discovered she was pregnant again, she decided to place this baby for adoption and join the Army Reserves. Her sister had agreed to take care of Elle's other children while she went away for training. She felt we were the right family to raise her daughter and asked to meet with us in person.

I'm not sure what I was expecting when she walked through the restaurant doors, but she was just the most precious girl. She sat down with us and we talked for hours. I found myself falling in love with her. I'd almost forgotten there was a baby involved here at all; I was just thrilled to be adding Elle to our family. CR and I listened intently as she told us her story and how she ended up in this situation; but, more important, she told us her dreams for her future and plans to change her life. She spoke with such authority and bravery, it was inspiring. The baby was due in a few short months, so we made plans to come back and visit Elle in a few weeks. We each had three other kids, and we decided that they should all meet as well. We thought it would be great to have a park playdate and let them all get to know one another.

Before the conversation ended, Elle let us know that there was one thing that really concerned her. Her mother didn't know Elle was pregnant again; her mom had a very "old school" way of thinking, Elle explained, and would not be okay with a baby being placed for adoption. While I couldn't imagine keeping a secret like that from my own mother, I also didn't have a toxic relationship with my mom, so I knew Elle was doing what she believed to be best in this situation. Elle assured us that this was what she wanted, though, and that she saw this adoption as an opportunity for a fresh beginning. She seemed so hopeful and excited, which is not at all what I would have expected.

We left dinner that night so full of emotion. I loved Elle already, and I could tell she was drawn to CR, which didn't surprise me because he's so likable and way less awkward than me in those situations. Maybe it was the forty-five cheese biscuits I nervously ate while she told us her story. Whatever the reason, she liked us and chose us to raise her baby, and we were honored.

CR and I talked the entire three-hour drive home about how incredible this all was, how we never expected to fall so in love with an expectant mama, and how we could just see God's goodness all over this situation.

God was finally bringing us our baby Rose, and I was determined to love her well, to do everything I could for her. I lovingly filled her little closet with tiny pink clothes, shoes, and tons of diapers. I'd also decided that I was going to try and lactate so I could nurse her. I knew a few other adoptive mamas who had nursed, and they all said it had been so beneficial for bonding. I rented a hospital-grade pump, looked up the protocol for this process, and began pumping every three hours around the clock until my body started to produce milk again. It was a super small amount, but everything I'd read said that once you had an actual baby to nurse, the milk production would pick up. I was all in: my heart was in it, my soul was in it, and now my body was, too. We were ready for a baby girl, baby Rose.

Elle called me one night to tell me she'd been in a small car accident. She assured me that she was fine and so was the baby, but she had to cancel our playdate with all the kids. I completely understood and offered to help in any way she needed. The due date was quickly approaching, and we'd kept in touch via text message as she prepared for delivery. The plan was to call us when she went into labor, and we'd make the three-hour drive to meet her at the hospital. She wanted me to be with her in the delivery room, and I was honored to be there with her as she brought this sweet baby into the world.

The week she was due, I went ahead and packed our "go bags," with everything we'd need for a few days out of town and all the baby things. I'd gone a tad overboard shopping for this baby, but it was the only way I could distract myself during the wait. We had all the arrangements for childcare, and my mom was at the ready to come over and watch Kennedy, Shelby, and Noah when the big day finally came.

Once again, I found myself stuck between two emotions. I was anxious and excited for the birth of this baby girl—I mean, I was going to be her mama. We were going to be her family. That feeling never came alone, though; like a rain cloud over my happy parade was the stark reminder that this day would be devastating for Elle. She would say goodbye to her baby girl that day. That thought, no matter the circumstances, ripped my heart out every time. Once again, God was asking me to hold two very different emotions at the same time—to just sit in the pain and the beauty together.

May 9 started like any other day. I got the kids dressed; we did our schoolwork and then drove to the strawberry patch to meet up with some friends. It was scorching hot that day, and after spending hours in the sun playing and picking strawberries we decided to take the kids out for some lunch and a cold iced tea. My friends peppered me lovingly with questions about Elle and the baby, and we all just soaked in the excitement of the days to come. The kids and I arrived home sticky with sweat but with full bellies and full hearts. I got the kids all settled in for rest time and headed downstairs to open a large package that had been dropped on the porch. I slid my knife over the tape and inside the box I found a sweet note written by CR's grandma and tons of baby clothes! It seemed that no one could resist spoiling this baby girl, even family that lived three thousand miles away. I unwrapped each piece and couldn't help but smile as I imagined a precious new baby wearing them. After I'd gone through each piece one by one and fawned over them all, I put the box on the dining room table, a landing zone for things that need to make their way upstairs but that I'm too tired to lug up there right at the moment.

I poured myself a glass of water and headed out back to our gazebo to just chill for a few minutes. Just as I sat down, the phone rang. It was our attorney. Excitement rushed over me. I just knew she was calling to tell us that Elle was in labor, that it was finally time!

I answered quickly, but the excitement in the attorney's voice did not match mine.

"I've got some bad news. Elle has changed her mind. She's decided to keep the baby. . . . I'm pretty sure she's already been born. I think her mother found out. I'll update you when I know more."

My phone slid from my hand and hit the gazebo floor, my body followed slowly. I lay there and wept. I didn't need to wait to hear more. I knew her mom had found out and stopped her from following through. Elle loved this baby so much, she loved all her kids so much, she wanted to rewrite her own story. I honestly didn't know how to feel. This was always Elle's baby; we would have considered it a great privilege to raise her if that was what Elle wanted, but this baby was never mine. For me, I needed to grieve what might have been, but I also grieved the loss of Elle.

We never heard from her again.

Our attorney confirmed weeks later that Elle's sister had told her mom about the baby, and Elle's mom put a stop to the adoption. My hope is that perhaps her mother had a change of heart and, instead of just stopping the adoption, she stepped up to help Elle. Maybe she agreed to take the children while Elle did her training? I pray Elle's story ended with her keeping her baby and her dreams.

This side of heaven, I may never know what became of Elle and her children. It's been five years since I last spoke to her, and in that time, those nearly two thousand days, I've never stopped praying for her. She changed my life more than she could ever know. She opened my eyes to see the complexity of what it means to be a "birth mom," though she never wore that title; she showed me how you can love someone so much that you're willing to let her go. I never knew her baby, but I knew Elle, and it was truly my honor to walk alongside her those few months.

When we first started the adoption process, I was afraid of doing an infant adoption. I was afraid of what it might be like to share a child with another woman, for a child to have two mamas in his or her life. Loving Elle made me see that it's really no different than a mama having more than one child to love. Your heart gets bigger, and there is only more love to give. I've learned that it's the same for a child as well. They can expand their hearts to love two mamas, too.

13

Jehovah Jireh

He calls us to trust Him so completely that we are
unafraid to put ourselves in situations where we
will be in trouble if He doesn't come through.

—Francis Chan

As the summer was coming to a close, we had taken months
to do the work of healing our hearts after our failed adoption. I was finally feeling ready to get back out there, to
open ourselves yet again, to what might bring us our baby
or what might bring us more pain. We let our adoption
consultant know that we were ready to begin presenting to
expectant mamas again.

On Saturday, October 12, at 8:59 p.m., I received an email
with a subject line that read, "Baby boy born Oct 6th."

The kids were all sound asleep, CR was watching TV

in the living room, and I was in my home studio editing pictures from a photo shoot I'd done earlier. I opened the email to find a lengthy explanation of the baby's story and a photo. It stopped me dead in my tracks. He was the most beautiful little baby, swaddled tightly, lying peacefully in a hospital bassinet. He was a tiny peanut weighing in at five pounds, fifteen ounces, and he had the most gorgeous full lips I'd ever seen on a baby. That feeling came swiftly, the one that came when God was assuring me I belonged in this story. I sprung from my chair and ran into the living room to show CR. I spoke quickly and excitedly about this baby boy who needed a family, and how he was already born, and how a family would be chosen as soon as possible, and how I thought we should have our profile shown as a potential family. He was a tad stunned since I just kind of ran in the room and word-vomited all over him. He paused and said, "Okay, that all sounds great, babe. How much are the fees?"

I started deflating like a popped balloon.

"Well, it's about $10,000 more than we have in savings right now, but I'm sure we can figure it out." The failed adoption had depleted many of our resources, and we hadn't yet built them back up.

His eyes got as big as a dinner plate. "If he's already born, don't we have to pay the money now?"

I could see I was losing him . . . and fast. "I mean, yeah, in like three weeks after court."

"I'm sorry, babe, I just don't see how we can come up

with $10,000 in just a few weeks. We spent a year pulling together the funds for Noah's adoption. I'm just not sure this is the right placement for us."

I reluctantly agreed, shuffling back into the office to edit. I exhaled loudly as I flopped back into my chair. Now I was just annoyed and kind of angry. I tried to edit, but I couldn't stop looking at the photo. I felt the tears building up. Was I just sad because I hate that money is a part of the equation at all? I tried to sort through my feelings, but I kept getting that nudge—that unshakable feeling. I dropped my head into my hands as the tears fell. That's when I heard Him, like a quiet whisper in my heart, asking, "Do you trust me?"

I'd spent all this time saying how I believed God would be faithful in what He called us to—how He loved these children more than I could and how money was nothing to Him. That's the beauty of His upside-down Kingdom. And now He was basically calling me out: "You say you believe I will provide, but only if you can see how. Where is your faith? Will you step off the cliff and trust that I will catch you?"

The stakes seem to get higher every time He leads me to a new cliff. He rarely asked super hard things of me as a new believer. I had opportunities left and right to practice stepping out in faith in small and seemingly inconsequential ways. But now, the chips were all being pushed into the middle. Was I in, or was I out?

I popped up out of my chair and charged back into the living room.

"Look, babe, I love you and I know you only want what's best for our family, but we have to try. God has provided us an open door and He's asking us to walk through it. I don't know what's on the other side. I don't know if we'll get chosen to be this little boy's parents. I don't know how we'll get the money. I just know we have to keep walking through the doors until there aren't any more left."

The look on my face or the sternness of my voice must have made it evident I'd already decided, because all CR said was: "Okay, babe, you're right. Let's just try."

That green light from CR was all I needed to hit the ground running. I fired off the email letting our consultant know we were in!

I knew an answer wouldn't come until Monday at the very earliest, so I did what any other control freak/ball of anxiety, who wants to trust but doesn't fully, would do. I started writing down ideas of all the ways we were going to come up with the money. Garage sale, mini photo shoots, bake sale, pancake breakfast, T-shirts, basically selling anything in our home that wasn't nailed down. I even broke down how much I thought we could realistically make from each thing to ensure we had a shot at hitting the $10,000.

I kept the baby's picture up on my screen to remind me what I was working toward, just in case we were chosen.

Monday rolled around and the day was nearly coming to a close when I called my sister to whine. I'd heard nothing all day and so I had already convinced myself that it must have meant bad news for us.

"I'm sure they chose someone else. It's fine, I'm fine," I sulked.

That's when the call waiting beeped in. It was a Florida number, which happened to be the state the adoption agency was in. I'm not even sure what I said to Ash, something like, "It's them. Florida. Gotta go."

I cautiously answered the call, and the woman on the other end was so kind. We chatted for a brief moment (which felt like an eternity) before she said the words I'll never forget: "You've been chosen for this baby boy. Congratulations!"

By this point I was hopping up and down on the sofa, trying to keep my voice calm while my body convulsed with excitement. We talked a little longer about logistics and time frames, and as I hung up, I glanced at the list on my desk. I was thrilled but also terrified. What if I just said yes, and we couldn't come up with the money? What if we lose him? I wanted to trust God, but I was crippled with fear.

When I told CR we were chosen, it was obvious he felt the same way. Overjoyed, but overwhelmed at what this really meant.

That night I stayed up late to craft a blog post about our newest addition. At the time, I had a small blog read only by family and friends in which I kept everyone up to date on our growing family and our adoption process. I poured my heart out in that post. I shared about how much we loved this baby boy already and how we were going to do everything we could to ensure he didn't spend one more day without a mama. I included all the details of the fundraisers we had planned, letting people know where they could donate garage sale items, buy T-shirts, or sign up for photography sessions. At the end of the post I included a link to our AdoptTogether account, which allows people to make tax-deductible donations toward a family's adoption if they want to help in that way. I set the post to go live the following morning.

I tossed and turned all night. I kept waking up just to look at the baby's photo to be sure that I hadn't imagined it all, that he was really going to be our son. In truth, I felt nervous, too. I knew when we announced his adoption we'd be met with some concerned responses, wondering whether it was responsible to move forward when we didn't have all the money and the time line was short.

When I could no longer stave off the voices of fear and misgiving in my mind, I gave in and got up for the day. I poured my coffee, made the kiddos breakfast, and sat down at my computer. I was stunned to see tons of congratulatory messages from friends and family. My inbox was filled with emails from people requesting to book photography sessions, asking to drop off garage sale items, and even offering us clothes and baby items we might need. What I did not expect, though, was the money being donated into our AdoptTogether account. A dollar, five dollars, one hundred dollars. My friends began sharing my blog post with their friends, who shared it with their friends, and so on. One woman in particular, whom I barely knew, seemed to make it her personal mission to see we had the funds needed. She was well connected and urged her friends to help—and they showed up, big time! Another family we knew, but not very well at the time, offered a $2,500 matching grant! We could not believe it! I must have sat at that computer desk all day with tears streaming down my face. I watched as dollar after dollar flooded in.

Not even twenty-four hours after I published my blog post, we had more than $11,000 in our AdoptTogether account. God took all my plans about how to get this money and blew them out of the water.

He used His people—His hands and His feet—to provide every last penny.

Jehovah jireh—God will provide.

God could have allowed this to drag on for three weeks, I could have held fundraiser after fundraiser, and maybe we could have pulled together the money, but I fully believe God wanted to show up and show off. He wanted to be certain there was no doubt, that I did not do this on my own power. God provided in a way that only He can.

In Matthew 14, when Jesus is walking on the water, He tells Peter to come to Him—to step out of the boat and walk on the water, too. Peter does the scary part and steps out of the boat, but with the first little whip of wind he doubts Jesus, gets scared, and begins to sink. As He always does, Jesus reached out His hand to catch Peter, saying, "You of little faith, why did you doubt?"

I don't know about you, but I want to be like Peter when

Jesus says, "Come." I want to get out of the dang boat. When Jesus calls me up I want to say, without hesitation, without fear, "Yes, Lord, I'll follow you anywhere!"

God has shown me time and time again, He doesn't want my hustle, He wants my heart. He wants me to be unafraid to walk into the hard places, to step off the cliff, to get out of the boat.

I did my best version of Peter on that Saturday night when the email came through, and Jesus asked me to step out of the boat. I said yes, but then, just like Peter, I let fear take over and I began to strategize how to do it all my way. He didn't need my help, though; He was more than prepared to do what He had promised. He asked me to walk through the open door and trust Him to provide. And while this miracle is one of my very favorite parts of our story, it's also the one that exposed a big stumbling block in my faith.

Growing up, I'd been taught that money is evil. I don't remember exactly when I first heard it, but over the course of my teen and young adult years I saw the great divide between those who had a lot of money and those who didn't. How many times have we heard the phrase "money is the root of all evil"? For that reason, I kept money separate from God. It was something necessary to live, but I didn't see anything holy about money.

Funding our adoptions forced me to take a long, hard look at what God actually has to say about money in the Bible. What I discovered is that God actually calls money a blessing, though the *love* of money is evil, since it becomes something we worship more than Him.

When used properly, money can do so much good. It can bless people.

What I've learned through first Noah's adoption, and then Jonah's, is that in this great commission of discipleship and sharing the gospel around the world, there are "goers" and there are "senders."

There will always be people who make more money, and there will be people who make little but have callings to do things that require money.

We need them both.

We need the people who run into the hard places: the ones who pastor the churches, the ones who say yes to being foster parents, the ones who adopt the special needs child everyone else has overlooked. The world desperately needs these "goers." But I've witnessed firsthand how we also need the people who have the resources to send the goers: those who can fund the work, pay the salaries, cover the expenses. This hurting world needs them both. How foolish I'd been to think that God's goodness could be contained in only one of those kinds of people.

We live in a fallen world, so none of this will ever be perfect. There will be so many mistakes, and I do believe money in the hands of a person with an evil heart will lead to destruction, but money in the hands of those who fiercely chase after the heart of God can be used for so much good.

Just a few days after this incredible miracle, I received

a call from our local news station asking whether a crew could come out and film a segment about our story. Reporters had seen our Facebook post and watched as the money quickly came in. They, too, were blown away at how our community rallied around us to bring our baby home. Once the segment aired, there were so many comments on the video from people who had donated. Many people said that for various reasons they could not adopt but had always wanted to. I couldn't believe what I was reading; these people actually thanked *us* for allowing them to be a part of our son's story through their donation.

All this time I believed this miracle was about us and our son. But God used it to bless perfect strangers as well. It gives me chills to think of what a loving God we serve. I may never know all those touched by that single decision to say yes to this door God opened, and I think that's the point. We don't need to know what's on the other side of every door He opens for us, we just need to trust Him.

Bringing Jonah Jeffrey, or JJ as we now call him, home a few weeks later was one of the most precious moments of my life. I'd driven late into the night to ensure we made it home to be together as a family for Thanksgiving. The kids begged to stay up late and meet their new baby brother. Kennedy and Shelby managed to stay awake but sweet little Noah just couldn't hang. I sat down on the sofa and gently passed baby Jonah to his oldest sister for a snuggle. Kennedy pulled his body tightly to hers and touched his face softly. Then she looked up at me with a bit of confusion. She had tears streaming down her face. "Mommy, why am I crying? I'm so happy, not sad."

I brushed her hair from her face and assured her that this was just what overwhelming happiness felt like—this was what it was to be so happy you cry.

Both girls spent the rest of the evening passing baby Jonah back and forth, fawning over him and arguing about who got to feed him and give him his pacifier back when it fell out of his mouth. Their love for him was instant.

The next morning, I waited anxiously for Noah to wake up. He had just turned two years old, and while we had talked so much about his new brother, I really didn't know what to expect when Noah actually met Jonah.

It wasn't long before I heard him stirring, and I ran up to his room to say good morning. As he rubbed the sleep from his eyes, I told him that his new brother, Jonah, was here and asked whether Noah wanted to go downstairs and meet the baby. A smile engulfed Noah's little face, and he ran for the door!

CR was in the kitchen holding his newest baby boy while I got Noah comfy on the couch. I put pillows under his elbows and hoped he wouldn't lose interest and toss the baby onto the floor. Noah at that age was such a loving, tenderhearted little guy, but he was also wild! He was always jumping off furniture and constantly running, so my concerns were pretty valid.

What happened next will forever be branded on my heart. I plucked Jonah from his daddy's arms and placed him on Noah's lap. Immediately Noah stopped wiggling and just sat there—calmly. He held Jonah so tightly while switching between giving Jonah kisses and pressing his own cheek against Jonah's face. Noah seemed overcome with love for his new baby brother. Over the years we've seen that this is just who Noah is. He loves babies, loves to snuggle them, and is so tender with them. It's like they melt his wild heart and bring him a sense of peace and calm.

Once again, I found myself in awe of God's beautiful plan for my life. I had a front-row seat to see how God was using each of these hard stories, these moments of heartbreak and doubt, these messy and broken pieces, and weaving them together into something so beautiful: a family.

Me in the
first grade.
I couldn't
read, but
wasn't I
cute?!

Ashleigh and me. I'm sure you
can guess which one is me.

CR and me just a few months before our wedding.

Our wedding day, August 2005.

Shelby as a newborn, and me as a new mama
of two girls under two years old!

Shelby and Kennedy
in 2009—my happy
and silly girls!

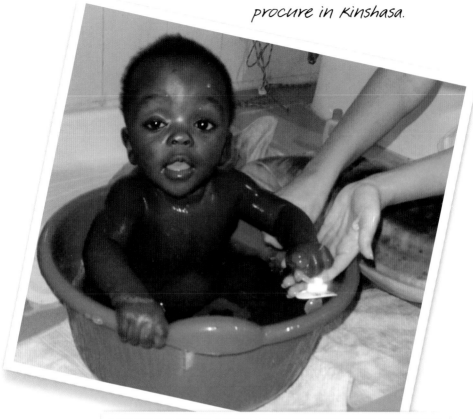

Noah's first bath at the procure in Kinshasa.

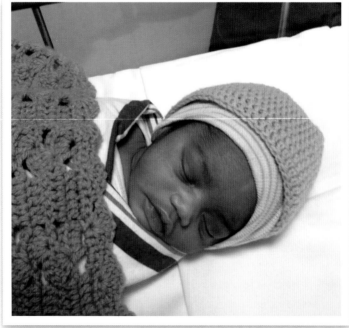

The first photo we saw of baby Jonah.

Noah meeting Jonah for the first time. He was instantly in love.

Jonah at four months old—the sweetest baby!

Two boys and two girls. For a minute we thought we might be done.

CR and the kids getting ready to cut down a Christmas tree!

Our family in 2015.

A few hours after we met Rosie, she was full of giggles.

Leaving the social welfare office with Rosie, both overwhelmed by emotions.

Rosie's first day home. She instantly loved her siblings, and they loved her right back.

My three musketeers.

Rosie's first time seeing the ocean—
she loved it!

Just a few
weeks after
Rosie came
home, this
was one of our
first outings
with all
five kids.

Twenty-eight-weeks pregnant with the twins, on our "babymoon" before becoming parents of seven kids!

Telling the kids we were having twins!

BABY A

BABY B

Exhausted but happy, the soundtrack of the first few months with twins.

The five big kids meeting the twins for the first time.

Ivy and Amelia, just a couple of weeks old.

our family of nine!

CR and baby Ivy—she was alert and so curious from the start.

Jonah and baby Amelia, my two free spirits.

Kennedy, Shelby, and the twins in our favorite place, Charleston, South Carolina.

The five big kids on our first camping trip with the new RV.

The kids in our new camper, ready to start our first adventure!

14

Infertility Begins

Motherhood: All love begins and ends there.

—Robert Browning

By 2014, we had four amazing children, which by society's standards was a big family and therefore should also
be a complete family. Our days were busy with lots of
little ones under foot, homeschooling, grocery shopping,
doctor's appointments, busy work schedules, and the hard
work of transitioning our newly adopted sons into their
home, but we were so happy. We'd really begun to let go
of any preconceived notions we had about what our lives
should look like, and CR and I both were embracing our
unconventional life.

My photography business was really taking off, and CR

was finally able to cut back from two jobs to just one. It was the first time in our entire marriage that he was actually home with us on the weekends. We spent the time together hiking, having picnics at the park, and just doing normal family stuff, but to us it felt like the big stuff we'd been missing out on when CR was gone all the time. Life was getting into a pretty good groove.

I narrowed my business down to be mostly focused on newborn photography. I've always loved babies and had a mild case of baby fever, but being around them all the time for work definitely kicked up the fever a notch or two.

During this time, I began to feel like someone was missing from our family. CR and I had always talked about having four kids as our maximum number of children, and we'd obviously reached that number, so we thought we were done at this point. I mean, we had two beautiful girls and two handsome boys. We felt so blessed that it almost seemed selfish to want any more children. But I couldn't shake the feeling.

It was more than just a feeling, too; there were times I'd load all the kids in the car and reach for a kid who wasn't there or grab an extra plate when serving up dinner. These were silly little things, and in the moment I'd laugh at myself, thinking I was just a busy mom who couldn't count and keep track of her kids. But in my heart I knew these were the little tugs, the ones that would leave me questioning whether we were really done growing our family.

For years I'd prayed that a cure for hyperemesis gravidarum (HG) would be found, and I would have the opportunity to conceive and carry a child again. After Shelby was born, we had resigned ourselves to the idea that HG would always be the stumbling block that prevented us from having more biological kids. God had called us to adoption, and we weren't sure whether He'd ever lead us back down the road of pregnancy again.

Adoption was never "plan B" for us, and having more biological children was never off the table, either. We listened to what we felt God was calling us to at the time and moved forward. The Bible is pretty dang clear that children are a blessing, so when CR and I felt God moving in our hearts to add another, we tried not to spend a ton of time questioning the hows and whys and whens; we just knew we needed to move out in faith. At this point we'd seen the fruits of allowing God to direct the steps in our life, and we were becoming stronger in our faith and more willing to just say yes, even when the path seemed full of unknowns.

One afternoon while the boys were napping and the big girls were watching a movie, I felt a pull to do some research. I began Googling cures and advances for hyperemesis to see whether there was any new information.

In my searching, I came across a private group on Facebook of women who were using a medication off-label to treat their HG, and it was actually working! Turns out, there was a doctor in New York who was doing some clinical

trials and finding this medication to be more than 98 percent successful in treating women who suffered from HG. I
felt a sense of hope and, dare I say, even excitement. Would
it actually be possible for me to carry a baby again? I called
everyone who knew me when I was pregnant with the girls,
who saw what I'd endured and could appreciate what a miracle this might be. I felt like God was really opening a door
here for us. CR and I talked through it all. I shared my copi-
ous amounts of research with him, and we both agreed the
next best step was to take it all to my former ob-gyn and
get his input before we did anything else.

I sat down on the edge of the exam table; the smell of al-
cohol swabs stung my nose a bit, but it was comforting in a
way. I never thought I'd be here again, in an ob-gyn's office,
talking about having a baby. I clutched the file folder tightly
as I answered the nurse's questions about insurance, what
pharmacy I used, and any allergies I had. It had been six
years since I'd been in this place and just the mere idea that
I might get to be here again as an expectant mama gave me
butterflies. My experience with HG was like a nightmare I
couldn't wake up from; it was a hell I wouldn't wish on my
worst enemy, but it was worth it all to have my children,
and the miracle of pregnancy and childbirth was something
my heart longed desperately to experience again. The idea
that I might get to experience this miracle without the
monster of HG gave me a hope to cling to, something I
had daydreamed about so many times, and now there was a
small chance it might be possible.

When the doctor came in it was like déjà vu; everything about him was so familiar. He greeted me warmly, but with a bit of a surprised look. I began speaking hesitantly, "I'm not sure if you remember me . . ."

He interrupted me. "Of course I remember you. You were one of the sickest patients I've ever had. I'm a little surprised to see you here!"

It's not exactly the way one hopes to be remembered, but maybe it would make it easier to convince him to let me try a medication still in clinical trials if he remembered me that way. I whipped out my folder and showed him all my research; I even think he was impressed. He told me it was obvious I'd looked into this extensively and that he would do his own research and get back to me, but it all looked very promising. I left his office on cloud nine.

I'm fairly certain I went home that night and started calculating due dates in case I got pregnant right away. I mean, we conceived Kennedy and Shelby within a month or two, so this would probably be super fast, too. I might have even started looking at baby names and pinning nursery decor on Pinterest. I was *all in*.

It didn't take too long for my doctor to call me back. Thankfully, he agreed that this medication was a great option for me and that he'd support me using it when I conceived again! Good gravy, this was actually going to happen. There are a few moments in my life when I felt such great happiness and joy that I can remember the moment vividly, and this was one of those moments. I can still close my eyes and bring myself back this feeling. I wasn't even pregnant. I didn't have any guarantee that the medication would work for me, but the anticipation, the belief, and the faith that the medication would work were enough.

I'd like to keep this book mildly appropriate should my children ever choose to read it one day, so let me just say this. CR and I began trying to conceive, we gave it our all, went at it with gusto, gave it the old college try—you get the point.

A few weeks later, I stood nervously over the bathroom counter while my pregnancy test was doing its thing. My heart was nearly beating out of my chest. This was going to be it; I could just feel it. For six years I struggled with the idea of never being pregnant again, never giving birth or breastfeeding. So many close friends and family never understood why I'd even want to be pregnant again, since pregnancy had been so rough for me before, and I could never adequately explain myself. Over the years I'd pleaded with God to take the desire away. It wasn't going to be possible, so I just wanted Him to take the feeling away. But He didn't. It would get tabled for a while during our adoption processes, but it was never gone for good. The desire was deep down in my soul; for a long time I'd allowed others' opinions to keep me from validating my desire. They thought I was a little crazy, and maybe I was, but I didn't need anyone's approval to desire another baby, and while I'd spent years asking God to remove that desire, He hadn't, and now I was being given a chance to try again.

Three minutes had passed and with a deep breath and a huge grin, I flipped the test over to see the result.

Negative.

The result stung, and I even felt a little embarrassed. I had been so sure that we'd gotten the timing right; I mean we had "tried" basically every freakin' day! Did we miss the window? Good Lord, how small was the window? Or maybe I was just testing a bit too early? I convinced myself that testing too early was the reason and dropped the negative test in the trash can. Surely it would be positive tomorrow.

But it wasn't. In fact, it wasn't positive the next day or the day after that or the day after that.

It wasn't even positive the month after that, or the month after that. For the next six months, every single test was negative.

There are women who try for years to conceive and so, while in my heart I felt something was wrong, I gave myself the "Stop complaining, pick yourself up by your bootstraps" speech and tried to carry on. Deep down, I knew this wasn't normal for me. I conceived quickly and easily with Kennedy and Shelby. Getting pregnant wasn't supposed to be the hard part for me. No, I was the girl who had crappy pregnancies. I was the one who puked countless times a day, I was the one who needed PICC lines and medication to survive while pregnant. I was *not* the girl who couldn't get pregnant to begin with. I felt anger creeping in.

It's not fair.

I didn't say it out loud, but I thought it many times.

It's not supposed to be this way.

Even my doctor thought it was strange and agreed to run some tests for us to make sure things were looking okay. When the results came in, it did little to ease my mind. Everything looked pretty good, CR's sperm count was a little low, but he'd been sick recently, and the doctor said illness could have an effect on those numbers. All in all, there was nothing that jumped out and said, *this*, this is why you haven't gotten pregnant! I think sometimes we actually want to find something wrong; we want an explanation, something that can be resolved or fixed. The unknown leaves too much space for our brains to conjure up ridiculous reasons that feed off of our insecurities:

I can't get pregnant again because I'm a bad mom to the kids I already have.

I've done something wrong, so God doesn't think I deserve another baby.

I'm being punished for something I did in my past.

As time passed and the negative tests piled up, it became harder and harder to silence the voices telling me this was a punishment or that pregnancy was a blessing I wasn't worthy of. All the hope I'd been holding on to was beginning to fade. All of the trust I had built up watching God do amazing and miraculous things to bring home Noah and Jonah began to fade. The still, small voice of God became buried under the noise of my fears and dashed dreams. It can be all too easy to forget that voice when doubt creeps

126

in. For me, it wasn't just doubt in "the plan" but doubt about what I felt God was telling me. I was questioning whether I was actually hearing from Him at all. Was that voice all in my head? Or had my own desires become so loud that they were drowning out God? I struggled to find the *kol demama daka*; the thin silence seemed to be out of reach. I wanted desperately to trust Him in spite of my own feelings.

As I dropped yet another negative test into the trash, through tears I whispered to myself, "And if not . . . He is still good."

15

Our Rose

I, the Lord, will make it happen in its time.

—Isaiah 60:22 (NLV)

I was unsure about what to do next and found myself questioning everything as another month passed and another batch of negative tests found their way into the garbage.

On a lazy afternoon, when we had no big plans for the day, I curled up on the couch and began my afternoon scroll. This was the time I'd just zone out reading Facebook posts, scrolling through Instagram photos, and checking my email. I couldn't tell you one single thing I saw or read that day until I was halted mid-scroll by a photo of the most adorable little girl I'd ever seen. It was posted by Stefanie, who was an advocate for children who were waiting to be adopted in China. Her blog, *No Hands but Ours*, was dedicated to resources for adoptive parents and advocating for children in China. She had written a post about this little girl, Rosie, who was three years old, had Down syndrome, and needed a family.

As soon as I saw her name, Rosie, I got that feeling again. Was this her? Was this our Rose? By this point I'd somewhat lost hope that she was real, that she ever existed in the first place. I'd pretty much convinced myself that either I'd heard God wrong a few years ago, or maybe I had made the message more literal than He had meant it to be. It had been almost four years since that name had been placed on my heart; we now had two sons and a failed adoption of a baby girl, so perhaps I'd just heard wrong.

I wasn't sure what to think, but I needed to know more. The blog post was so beautifully written and shared all about Rosie's spunky personality. While there were unknowns about her, the one thing that was without question was that she needed a mama. Toward the end of the post Stefanie shared the contact information for the agency that had Rosie's file. Without any hesitation, I fired off an email. What could it hurt just to ask, you know?

When CR arrived home from work, I shared with him all about this darling little girl. I showed him her name, hoping he would see the same connection I did. He agreed to find out more, but he was honest in telling me he needed more time to consider all this. For better or worse, CR likes to stick to what he's started. He doesn't love changing mid-course, and all this time we'd been on a path to have another biological child. Adoption hadn't even been a discussion at that time; it wasn't anywhere on the radar. I know the idea took him completely off guard, which is fair.

However, I tread lightly if I start to question God's timing when I feel He is calling us to adoption. It's easy to make it all about us, to complain about the timing or to worry that we're just not in that "headspace" right now. There are myriad excuses we use to explain away our indifference, but there is one simple thing God reminds me every time I try to whine to Him about timing. It's never the right time for children to lose their parents, to be abandoned, to become orphans. They didn't ask for this, and they did nothing to deserve it. They need someone to say an emphatic "yes!" to them, someone to love them unconditionally.

I had plans to go away for the weekend with a few of my mama friends for a little trip we like to call "Moms Gone Mild." Once a year, we spend a weekend lying around a beach house like a bunch of slugs, stuffing ourselves silly with guacamole and pimento cheese dip. It's just as glorious as it sounds.

I'd been talking with Rosie's caseworker at the agency, and we had some paperwork to fill out before they would let us view her file. I completed the paperwork as fast as I could and then waited rather impatiently for the file to appear in my email. It was late Friday afternoon when the email finally came, and we were already at the beach house for our getaway.

Unfortunately, my phone couldn't open the .zip file attached to the email, so I would have to wait until I got home to look it over. I tried to be patient, which is one virtue among many others that I do not possess, and I asked my friends to pray for us and for this little girl. I didn't know what was going to happen. I knew CR was uncertain and that this was all new territory for us. I didn't know much about Down syndrome. I knew I wasn't afraid of it, but I didn't have a lot of firsthand experience with it, and I wasn't sure whether perhaps I was just being naive.

Monday morning rolled around. I was home and settled from my trip, CR was at work, and the kids were doing schoolwork when I sat down at my computer to sift through Rosie's file. It was written in both Mandarin and English, so it took me a few moments to get my bearings on what exactly I was reading: intake papers, medical history, and updates from the orphanage staff on her progress. I noticed in the upper right-hand corner my birthday was listed. Why was my birthday on the file? That seemed strange. And then I looked at the year: 2011.

I just sat there, frozen.

I felt a single tear fall and a feeling that can only be described as a warm hug from the Father wash over me. That wasn't my birthday; it was Rosie's. She and I shared a birthday, July 30. As beautiful and incredible as that was, it wasn't that part that brought the tears. She was born in *July 2011.* The same month and year that God had told me I had a daughter, and that her name would be Rose, was the exact same month and year that this sweet girl was born half a world away.

I crumpled to the floor, in awe of what an incredible God we serve: a God of details, a God who writes the most intricate and beautiful love stories and then sees fit to include us in them. He allows us to be a part of them, and that honor is one I never get tired of receiving.

There she was, *my Rose.*

I thought she'd be Congolese, but then God brought us Noah. I thought she'd be a newborn baby, but then God brought us Jonah. All this time, God knew exactly who she was, a beautiful Chinese girl made extra special, precious in His sight. Every single step, every joy, and every heartbreak had conspired together to bring us here—to bring us to each other.

Sometimes we want so desperately to hit the fast-forward button, to get to the end result quickly and painlessly. In reality, the timing had to be this way. When Rosie was born and brought to the orphanage, CR and I were both twenty-seven years old. The Chinese government requires parents to be thirty years old in order to begin an adoption. CR and I were now, finally, thirty years old. As much as I wish we could have been with her from the beginning, this was the way the timing worked out to make Rosie a part of our family. God primed my heart so many years before so that when the timing was right, we'd be ready and willing to burst through the open door to go and get our Rose.

It seemed there was no decision left to make, I knew what God was doing, and I was ready to go get my daughter. It all sounds a bit like a fairy tale, right? But that's not real life. Despite the signs that were so clear in my eyes, my darling husband still had reservations. I wanted so desperately for him to see this as I did, a perfectly laid-out plan by God; but the truth was, he needed some time to confer with God himself.

CR asked me for a few days to think about it. The challenges of raising a child with Down syndrome were scary—the unknowns, the future for her and for us. CR understandably wanted some time to consider it all. The logical side of my brain couldn't blame him for needing this time, so I did my best to back off for a few days. My best was pretty pathetic though. I just couldn't keep the smile off my face, and I even bought Rosie an adorable dress I found on clearance. After a day or two of my annoyingly peppy attitude and unshakable assurance, he came to me and through a slight grin and half laughing he said, "Of course she's our daughter. Let's go get her."

On average, the process to adopt from China takes about a year. One day I met up with a friend who knew all about the process it takes to complete a Chinese adoption, so I knew I could pepper her with questions and she'd likely know the answers.

"What's the fastest you've ever seen someone get through the paperwork and get their child home?" I asked.

My friend hesitantly replied, "Well, um, without a medical expedite, I'd say maybe nine or ten months?"

With a smug grin I told her, "Great. I'm getting Rosie home in eight months."

I wish I could find the words to explain what it's like to be holding a photo of your child and know that all that stands between you is the completion of some paperwork and signatures. I mean sure, the process is vastly more complicated than that, but to a mama's heart, it could be climbing Mt. Everest, and we'd still look it square in the eye, and say, *"Bring it on."* Rosie had been waiting years and my heart couldn't handle her waiting even one single day longer than was absolutely necessary.

I kept meticulous binders with notes on how to complete each step as quickly as possible. There was a divider for each approval needed, the date it was expected and the date I was pushing to have it done by, which was often days or weeks ahead of schedule. I filled out form after form, updated our home study, and ran back and forth getting medical evaluations for our whole family. While all this was exhausting, each box I checked was bringing us one step closer to our daughter. This was the kind of box-checking I could get behind!

We were fortunate that Rosie was living at a non-governmental organization (NGO) run by a group called International China Concern (ICC). She was receiving excellent care; they even arranged things so that the kids lived in small family groups with one or two steady caregivers to help them have a more normal family structure. This arrangement also helps immensely when children are adopted, as they have some sense of family life. We received tons of photos of Rosie dating all the way back to her infancy. It was amazing to have these not only for us, but for Rosie, too. Many children who spend years in an orphanage will never have any photos of themselves as a baby, so we knew this was a special gift for both of us. As we waited for paperwork and approvals, we received new photos almost monthly and even the occasional video of Rosie. I loved watching her grow and change but, man, I wanted to be there with her instead of watching it all from across the world.

Toward the end of the process, we were allowed to send her a small care package. We filled the box with a small blanket I'd slept with for a few days so it would have my scent on it. When I first heard of this idea, I thought it sounded kind of silly, but scent is our strongest memory recall, and I was willing to do whatever I could to ease the pain for Rosie in the first few days when she would be leaving everything she'd ever known. We also included a photo album with pictures of CR and me, the kids, and even our pets. We labeled them in Mandarin so the nannies could help her learn everyone's names and at least help her to know who I was when the big day finally came.

I first read about Rosie on Facebook in April 2015. Just a hair over eight months later, on Christmas Day of the same year, I boarded a plane to Beijing, China. It was time to get my girl.

16

On Being Brave

To be yourself in a world that is constantly
trying to make you something else is
the greatest accomplishment.

—Ralph Waldo Emerson

The first leg of the flight to China was quick and easy. My
sister Ashleigh traveled with me this time, after CR and I
agreed that we wanted him to use his vacation time from
work once Rosie was actually home and we were getting the
whole family settled and adjusted. We were preparing to
board the fourteen-hour flight from DC to Beijing, anxious
about the long flight and what would await us on the other
end, when the airline agent called my name over the loud-
speaker. I approached the desk nervously, and the agent
asked for my ticket. I slid it over the counter to her, and

with a blank face she said, "Here's your new ticket. You've been upgraded to first class."

You could have knocked me over with a feather! I ran back to Ashleigh waving our first-class tickets over my head like we'd won the lottery, which we basically had. Have you ever been in first class on an international flight? They give you these pods to sleep in. If you're a stomach sleeper then let me tell you, it's freaking glorious! The seat reclines totally flat and I was able to sleep about eight hours of the fourteen-hour flight. International travel is stressful by itself, but coupled with the nerves I felt about finishing the adoption process in a foreign country, being able to rest my body and mind on the way over was a huge help.

The real hero here is a dear sweet woman I'd met years before. When I interned at Intel in high school, I'd stayed in touch with one of the women I had worked for. She'd followed our family online and had always been so supportive of our adoptions, even hiring me to take photos of her kids when I flew to Oregon to do a fundraiser for Noah's adoption. When we announced we were adopting Rosie, she generously offered to pay for Rosie's flight home from China! Because she had all our flight information to ensure Rosie's ticket was booked with ours, she also put us on the upgrade list if first-class seats became available. I never could have predicted how an acquaintance from high school would play a part in all three of our adoptions!

After a couple long days of travel, we finally made it to Rosie's province, which meant I was only one sleep away from meeting my daughter. I laid out my clothes for the next day and carefully packed a little backpack I'd brought with me with some new toys and Chinese snacks we'd purchased from the market across the street.

As this was only my second time out of the United States, I was in awe as we made our way around the city. The hustle and bustle were intense, the buildings were massive, and the food was amazing! Even the quick street food and snacks from the market were so flavorful. I knew one thing for sure: Rosie was going to be wildly disappointed when she tasted the American version of Chinese food after eating the real stuff her whole life!

The next morning, we made our way downstairs to grab a bite to eat and then meet our guide who would take us to the social services office where I'd be meeting Rosie. The breakfast buffet in our hotel was incredible, like nothing I'd ever seen, but my nerves wouldn't let me eat. I couldn't stop thinking of how Rosie was just four years old and was going to be asked to leave everything she'd ever known and go with a stranger. Sure, I knew that the best place for Rosie wasn't an orphanage, no matter how good the orphanage was. I knew that all children belong in families where they can flourish. But children know only what they know. Rosie knew only her orphanage: good or bad, it was what was familiar to her.

As I sat there thinking, I was struck by what it must be like for children to be told they are going to live somewhere else, with complete strangers. It may feel a bit like being kidnapped—which is strong language to use—but I believe we parents need to thrust ourselves into the pain our children are experiencing to have any hope of understanding their reactions, which otherwise might not make a lot of sense to us.

As our guide led us to the orphanage, we were told that Rosie knew we were coming and that she seemed ready to be with her family. Even so, I tried to go in with no expectations of Rosie at all. The questions swirled around my brain: Would she let me hold her? Would she spit in my face and run screaming the other direction? Would she just be unresponsive? Any or all of those would have been a perfectly normal response to such a traumatic experience.

Our guide led us up to the second floor of the social services building and into a large room that was relatively empty. Inside was a couch and a coffee table against one wall. I perched myself on the sofa and anxiously rubbed my hands together while keeping my eyes on the elevator door. Rosie could be here any minute. Ash paced around the room and peered out the windows to catch the first glimpse of her car pulling up.

"It's her, I think it's her . . ." Ashleigh said excitedly. My heart was beating so fast I thought it might jump right out of my chest. I heard the "ding" of the elevators and watched as the gold doors slid open. A couple of men entered the room and one of them, the orphanage director, had Rosie in his arms. I slowly stood up and walked to meet them in the center of the room. The man holding Rosie noticed she had a runny nose, and he turned back to find a tissue. They were quite insistent that Rosie be in tip-top shape when I met her. They all scurried around trying to find a tissue. I looked at our guide and told her, half laughing, "I don't care about her runny nose, it's okay."

She spoke to the men in Mandarin and they turned back around to bring her to me. I approached her very slowly and made a little peace offering: a lollipop. The universal love language of all kids is candy. Rosie was visibly nervous, but she seemed to know who I was. The man handed her to me, and I gently brushed her hair back, trying to use body language to assure her everything was okay.

It took only a few moments for Rosie to warm up to me. We sat down on the couch, and she began to unload the contents of the backpack I'd brought her. She had come with her own little backpack from the orphanage, and inside it was the photo album I'd sent months ago. We flipped through it together, pointing out everyone, and I was a bit shocked to learn she had all the names memorized. She pointed to the photos as if she were explaining to *me* who the people in them were. Eventually Ashleigh came closer, and our guide explained to Rosie that this was her "ayi," or auntie. She would point to me and gleefully say, "Mama," and then she'd whip her finger over to Ash and with a slightly more stern tone say, "Ayi."

We had been a little worried that, if we brought two women into Rosie's life at the same time, she might be confused about which one of us was her mama. Over the next two weeks, Rosie made it abundantly clear that she knew *exactly* who her mama was, and that person was not Ashleigh. In fact, on the second day I began to run a very high fever, my body ached, and I could hardly carry our bags onto the train. I really needed Ashleigh to help me with Rosie, but my little Ru would have nothing to do with her. If Ash even tried to hand her a toy she'd fuss at her, "No, Ayi . . . Mama!" Even when I took a shower, there she sat, little Rosie Ru, right outside the shower door playing with her toys on the floor. She never left my side—not in a panicked, clingy way, either, but in a matter-of-fact way that just said, "This is my person."

The next step in the process was to go to the capital city of the province, Guangzhou, where every adoptive family comes to complete the final phase of their adoption. Unfortunately, even after my fever dissipated, I began having vertigo-like symptoms. We'd spent twenty hours on planes and a few more on a bullet train (yes, it's as fast it sounds), and my body couldn't seem to grasp that it was on solid ground now. I was light-headed and nauseated, and when I walked, it felt like I was on one of those moving sidewalks you find at the airport.

The next two weeks in Guangzhou were rough. I never really felt better, and while Rosie was doing so much better than I could have ever hoped for, she had her struggles, too. She'd never spent much time outside the walls of her orphanage, and so everything was new to her. For obvious reasons, she just didn't understand the expectations for her behavior in stores or restaurants, or even walking down the street. We'd walk through a store and she would stick her little arm out and drag everything off the shelf onto the floor. She would throw her food, hit random people walking by, and yell for what seemed to be no reason at all. I've always had pretty firm expectations of good behavior from my kids, especially in public, so this behavior was hard for me. But I gave Rosie as much grace as I possibly could, knowing she had been through so much and was just trying to make sense of it all.

What made it harder was the general attitude toward Rosie from the people we encountered each day. There's not much, if any, place in Chinese society for a girl with Down syndrome. There are hundreds of children in Chinese orphanages with Down syndrome waiting to be adopted; eventually, many of them move into adult mental institutions. While I had learned this fact before arriving in China, seeing that attitude in person was a harsh reality to confront.

I was shocked by how many times I was asked whether I was sure I wanted her. It was hard for me to understand a culture that seemed to see no value in her life, because to me, Rosie is an amazing child created in the image of God, worthy just as she is. And while the attitudes surrounding disability may be a bit better in the United States, we don't get it perfect, either.

Between feeling ill, adjusting to Rosie's transition, finishing the adoption proceedings, and navigating the cultural differences, the weight of everything felt heavier than I could carry. We ended up skipping many of the planned outings and stayed tucked away in our hotel room. I knew Rosie needed the bonding time, and I was growing increasingly more homesick by the day. Unlike my trip to Africa, this trip was much shorter and had a finite end date, and yet I was finding it so much harder.

As I reflected on what was missing, I realized that while I had made incredible connections with people in the Democratic Republic of the Congo (DRC), for various reasons that never really happened in China. From the time we adopted Noah, it was crucial to CR and me that we understand our children's cultures as best we can and help them as they grow to be confident in who God created them to be and where they come from. I'd been able to learn so much about the DRC from the people I met there, and I knew I needed to make an effort to bridge the gap of understanding here in China. Rosie was worth making that extra effort.

Little by little, I made the connections I was longing for. We experienced longer, deeper conversations with our guide, in which we learned about her family, her son, her hopes and dreams. Even a seemingly simple chance encounter with an elderly woman in the park began to help me see the humanity in a culture I just didn't understand. These encounters with people reminded me that we don't have to understand people to love them. We can make peace with the idea that we may see things differently and yet all bear the image of God.

After two weeks in China, our stay had come to an end and we made our way back to the States. The flight home was far less glamorous than the ride over. No first-class ticket this time, and a toddler who seemed to wait patiently for me to finally drift off to sleep before she began chucking all of our belongings at the people in the rows ahead of us. Turns out people don't like to be hit in the head with peanuts, toys, juice cups, or any other number of objects that Rosie found she could throw. This was a habit that would take close to a year for Rosie to outgrow. She quickly earned herself a nickname in our house: "Throwsie."

Throwing things was just one of the negative habits Rosie brought home with her. I never want to paint the picture that adoption is all sunshine and roses. It's born from loss and pain, and with those comes trauma. Bringing a total stranger into your home and asking everyone to just love one another immediately is unrealistic. In the years since, I've learned how vitally important it is to go into an adoption with eyes wide open.

But at the time, I hadn't learned that lesson yet. I figured that since Noah and Jonah had glided so easily into our family, Rosie would do the same. In many ways she did. But there were struggles, too. This was the first time we'd adopted a child older than a baby, and she'd lived a lot of life in her short four years, creating habits and behaviors that we had to learn to work with. There were dark days, and at times we questioned whether we'd made the right decision. Could we be good parents for her? Could we handle her needs? She was essentially ripped from all she'd known and asked to live a totally different life. Smells were all new, food was all new, even little things like having pets in our home were all new to Rosie. Given the circumstances she adjusted like a champ and embraced her new home and life with an open heart, ready to let us all in and love her. That's not always the case for kids who are adopted. We were so grateful to see her resilience, but we weren't immune to the struggles that come from such a massive change for our family.

In the weeks that followed Rosie's coming home I found myself in the darkest place I'd ever known. Even though, on the outside, everything seemed to be going fine, I found that depression and darkness don't care if everything in your life's going great. Depression can swallow you up whether there's a good reason for it or not.

I reached out to two women I barely knew, whom I'd spoken to a few times during our adoption process, as they also had little girls they'd adopted from China with Down syndrome. I was brutally honest with them. I shared my darkest feelings and thoughts, and they listened without judgment. They surrounded me and loved me through a time I couldn't even share fully with my own husband. They quite literally walked me off the ledge and helped me regain my sanity. By the grace of God, this was a short-lived time in my life and one that I was able to come out of quickly, but it's so important to surround yourself with people who love you and are invested in you and your family, and even more so when you're going through difficult times. We don't have to walk this road alone. These two women lifted me up, and I'm so thankful for them.

Rosie taught our entire family how to live. We were happy before, but she came in like a little ray of light and gave us all a new lens to see life through. She and the boys became our little three musketeers, always finding some mischief to get into, keeping us laughing. We learned to celebrate the little victories, the things we'd overlooked before. We learned to laugh at things that otherwise might have annoyed us. She is a child so filled with joy it's utterly infectious.

People often ask why we chose to adopt a child with Down syndrome. Frankly, I didn't spend a whole lot of time pondering all the what-ifs that made her different when Rosie came into our lives, and I'm glad I didn't. Rosie is just like the rest of my kids—she can be grumpy, extremely sassy, and hardheaded, but she's funny, she's adventurous, she's loving, and she's forgiving. She has a spark in her eyes that gives her a little something extra, something special.

When we told the kids we were going to adopt Rosie, and we shared with them that she had a special need, we held our breath to see how they'd respond. They asked a few questions, which we answered as best as we could, and then they responded, "Great! When is she coming home?"

It's amazing what we can learn from children. They don't put the same qualifiers on love and relationships as we do. My kids have all accepted one another as siblings from day one. They've made "Welcome Home" posters and cheered at the bottom of the airport escalator each time I've arrived home with their new brother or sister. They've shared their rooms, their toys, and their love without hesitation. Adults could take a few lessons from children about what it actually looks like to love without parameters. We are living in a time when the current cultural narrative is that kids are a burden or that they hold you back from your dreams, but I'd argue that children are the exact opposite. Children are the expression of everything that is beautiful and right in this world. They are joy and light and grace and forgiveness, and they love in a way we should all aspire to.

Sometimes God gives us blessings that we wouldn't ordinarily choose for ourselves, and I am thankful He chose us to be Rosie's family. She has taught me about living without fear, living in the moment, and what it really means to be brave. And she keeps our family laughing and living life to the fullest in a way we never had done before.

17

Just One More...

Children are a blessing and a gift from the Lord.

—Psalm 127:3 (CEV)

I was hesitant to share that we were still trying to have a baby after Rosie came home. Rosie wasn't ever meant to be a replacement for the child I'd had on my heart; Rosie was an "and." Adopting her came as a huge surprise to us, but God knew, and even while we were in the process to complete her adoption we made the decision to keep trying for a biological baby once Rosie was home and settled.

I've found that in terms of societal acceptance, there are unstated "rules" about how many kids you can have. If you don't have kids, you're selfish; have only one kid and you're spoiling him or her; two kids is perfect; three kids is pushing it; by four kids people start to ask if you "know what causes this"; and beyond that—well, people just assume you've lost your mind, and they act as though you have a hundred kids.

It's hard for me to understand the mentality that says children are a burden. Why is something God directly calls a blessing seen as an inconvenience? I know that not everyone is in the same situation we are and that there are difficult circumstances in which people are struggling financially and can hardly feed their kids, or single moms who have to work multiple jobs to make ends meet, with no spare time for themselves. But this is about a very typical attitude toward children that is pervasive in our society. When you tell people you got a promotion at work and a pay raise, you're likely met with excitement and encouragement. You're "#blessed" (*insert eye roll*).

But tell someone you're pregnant with your sixth child? Or tell them you're adopting a special needs child? The response is more like "Are you nuts?" Or my favorite: "Oh, wow, you must be vying for sainthood!" (And, yes, I've heard these and many more!)

The reactions we got from people as they watched our family grow didn't change the fact that we still felt like someone was missing from our family, and after we'd settled in with Rosie for a few months, we were ready to jump back into the TTC (trying to conceive) world. We decided to make an appointment at a local fertility clinic to get some blood work done and make sure there wasn't something we were missing. Most of our tests came back fine; some results were a little borderline, but nothing stuck out as a glaringly obvious reason we weren't conceiving. The doctor recommended we try a few rounds of intrauterine insemination (IUI), which basically involves taking the sperm, spinning them around a bunch, disorienting them, and then shooting them up your woo-ha with a big turkey baster. Okay, that's not exactly the process—but close enough.

We did that procedure three times over the course of the spring and summer, and every single time the result was a big fat negative. Our doctor was a bit dumbfounded; everything on paper showed we should have been able to conceive. We had two biological children already, so they knew it wasn't an issue of incompatible DNA. Our numbers looked pretty good—not stellar, but I was always a B student anyway. Things just didn't add up. The doctor sat us down and said with great confidence, "If you guys do IVF [in vitro fertilization] you will likely get pregnant on the first try."

Well, if you dangle that carrot in front of a woman who has been praying and trying to make this dream a reality for years, it's pretty likely she'll say yes. At this point I'd had more sex with my husband than should be possible in the course of each month. And you should know, TTC sex is not like regular sex. It's perfectly timed; only certain positions are allowed; and afterward you lie there with your legs up. After a while it feels more like a scheduled appointment than a frisky romp in the hay. Even CR grew tired of the calendar sex. By this point I'd also had a lovely nurse inseminate me when my husband wasn't even present. No one cuddled me or got me a snack, they just shot the sperm up there, gave me a bill to pay, and sent me on my way—not exactly how one might envision conceiving a child. Needless to say, I was open to the IVF discussion.

I know IVF is a complicated issue, and people have different perspectives about it. I've talked to people who think IVF is ethically wrong because they believe it's playing God. I understand why people feel this way, but I don't think it's really any different than any other form of modern medicine we use. When someone is diagnosed with Type 2 diabetes, we treat them. We give them medicine to help them be healthy. But when someone is diagnosed with infertility, we judge them harshly if they accept the help of modern medicine to conceive. The truth about IVF or any other procedure to get pregnant is that the outcome is always ultimately in God's hands. There are still no guarantees that IVF will result in pregnancy. God is still the only one who can breathe that spark of life into your body and create a pregnancy. As a photographer of mostly newborns, I've had many clients who conceived with the help of fertility treatments. Having seen those precious little faces and the love their parents had for them, I'll never be convinced that those babies aren't gifts to their parents and blessings from the Father, just like any other child.

We decided to move forward and do one and only one round of IVF. We made it very clear that we wanted a very conservative approach, as we knew we were going to have to make a plan for any embryos created during our IVF process. This meant that the embryos we didn't use this time would have only a few options. One option was to be discarded, which we weren't okay with; another was to be donated to a family, which we weren't sure we would ever be able to actually follow through with. They could also be donated to science, another no for us; and, finally, they could be used by us. We felt strongly that whatever embryos were created we wanted to be given a chance at life.

I called Ashleigh and filled her in on everything, and before I could tell her our full plan, she jumped in and offered to carry any of the embryos that I could not. If the medications didn't work, if my hyperemesis was too bad, she'd give our little frozen babies a chance at life. I knew she loved being pregnant, I knew it was relatively easy for her, but still, I was humbled that she would even consider doing that for us, let alone offer without me even asking. I felt so much peace and confidence that this was going to work out.

The leaves were changing, the air was getting cooler, and the arrival of fall meant it was time to begin our IVF protocol. For weeks I gave myself multiple shots in the butt and took various forms of pills as well. The nurse suggested I have CR do the shots, since it's a tough angle to reach yourself. You know how long that idea lasted? One. Single. Day. Poor dude was shaking and sweating, and I think I spent more time trying to keep him calm and boost his confidence than it would have taken me to just do the shots myself. By the time he'd mustered up the courage, my anxiety was at an all-time high, and the fact that he slowly drove the needle in instead of delivering a quick jab sealed the deal for me. I loved him, but he was fired from his job as my nurse.

I relieved CR of his duties and just did the dang shots myself for the next few weeks. If you ever see a woman who can't seem to sit down or is walking like she's got a stick up her butt, go easy on the judgment. She might be two weeks into an IVF protocol. My backside looked like it was losing every night at the underground fight club, and it felt like that, too. My hormones were all over the place. I'd go from crying to laughing in a matter of seconds, and my normally short(ish) fuse had become nonexistent. I was not pleasant to be around. Good thing it's a relatively quick process to go through, or poor CR might not have survived it.

The day arrived—egg retrieval day! After the procedure, we were told we had nine good-looking eggs ready to be fertilized. We were thrilled. We knew all nine wouldn't turn into viable embryos, but we were so hopeful that we'd get a few to use from this cycle.

Over the course of the next few days, the lab called us with updates. They'd tell us how many fertilized, how many were growing well, and other useful information. We prepared to go back in just a few days to transfer the best two embryos. Our doctor felt it was best to do a fresh transfer of two and then freeze the rest.

It was right around Jonah's birthday, so I'd stopped off

that morning at the grocery store to grab some cupcakes for him to share with his preschool friends that day. While I was in the produce section, my phone rang. It was the lab calling. I answered excitedly, but the doctor on the other end didn't have good news. Only two embryos were still viable, and they didn't look very good. After five days of growing in the lab, embryos should be at a phase of development when they're considered blastocysts. All our others had quit growing altogether, and these last two hadn't reached the "blast" phase yet as the doctors had hoped. We needed to transfer them both that day and just hope for the best.

I couldn't believe things had started out so well, and now we were being told this wasn't likely going to work.

I cried through the entire transfer. My doctor tried to encourage me to be positive, but in my heart of hearts I knew this was going to fail. I did everything she asked of me afterward. I drank plenty of fluid, stayed in bed for a few days, prayed and begged God to let just one of the babies "stick." The doctor doesn't have you come back in for blood work and a pregnancy test for a good two weeks after the transfer. There was no way I was going to be able to wait that long. I started taking at-home pregnancy tests about a week after, and, as I suspected, they were all negative. The blood work would eventually confirm what we already knew.

Our IVF procedure had failed.

At our follow-up appointment, the doctor told us that

the whole team had met to review our file, and as they did so, they discovered that one of my numbers was really off—something they hadn't noticed before. They wanted to do more blood work just to be sure. The results from that new round of blood work confirmed that I had the egg quality of a woman in menopause. Basically, I had crappy eggs, and the chances of us getting pregnant were very slim.

I'm a firm believer that some of these incredibly painful things are meant to prime us for the beautiful things that are coming. In this case, I'm not sure I would have been ready to say yes to what we did next if I hadn't already known what to expect with IVF and with embryo transfers; I even had an intimate knowledge of the heart behind a family's decision to do this procedure.

I had read about using donor embryos and had even seen an acquaintance talk about doing it herself. So during our "failure" meeting with our doctor, I mentioned the idea to her. We knew the issue was my eggs, and so using donor embryos would circumvent that problem altogether. My doctor wanted to talk the idea over with the team of other doctors and see what they all thought about the possibility of this option for us.

While I waited to hear back from the doctor, I did what I do best: research!

I found a gold mine of information about embryo adoption or donation. The terms are used interchangeably, though I quickly learned it is much more of a donation situation than an adoption one. As I'd felt many times before, something was telling me this was the right thing for us. At the end of the day, the baby's not being our genetic child wasn't a deal breaker for us. We wanted another baby, and I wanted another chance at a "normal" pregnancy; this option made all of that possible for us. It just felt right. Despite how wildly out of the norm it was, it seemed to be a really great option. Besides, we'd grown pretty accustomed to being seen as the weird family.

I was in the bookstore one morning when the doctor called me to inform me that the team had met, and they all agreed this could be a really great way for us to grow our family given the results of my testing and our failed IVF.

This type of adoption was different from anything we'd done before. On paper, it was basically like using an egg donor or a sperm donor, except you are essentially using both. When the baby is born there is no adoption process to go through. Your name is on the birth certificate as the parent, and as far as the government is concerned, legally, this is your baby.

It didn't take us long at all to match with a set of two embryos. Since numbers and dates have always played a big role in how I felt God was confirming things for me, when we got the paperwork about these two embryos and read that they were frozen three years before on October 12, 2013, I was amazed to see that this was the exact same day we received the email about a baby boy born in Florida who needed a family. That baby was our Jonah, and we felt more sure than ever that one or maybe even both of these embryos were our next little blessings. We decided to transfer both embryos at the same time. This was our last shot. We had multiple failed IUIs and a failed IVF, and this was it. We were at the end of the line—this was our Hail Mary, our last hurrah. If this didn't work, we felt ready to close the door on trying to conceive. The doctors all agreed it was best to transfer both embryos and just pray that one of them would "stick."

18

Seeing Double

Sometimes miracles come in pairs.

—Unknown

"Are you sure you didn't take any kind of an HCG [the pregnancy hormone] trigger shot before your embryo transfer?" the nurse asked. "No, we did a natural cycle. Are my numbers really high?" I questioned.

"Well, yeah, they are. Let me talk to the doctor, and I'll have her call you," she replied.

There was no need for the doctor to call me. I knew it. Both embryos had "stuck," and we were having twins. I'd already prepared myself for the transfer not to work at all. If you've ever struggled with anxiety, then you know what happens next. That train came rolling into town and brought with it all this nonsense that sent me into a tailspin.

Your body can't do this.

You're basically Michelle Duggar now.

Seven kids is way too many kids.

You won't be able to carry these babies to full term.

People are going to judge you so hard for having so many kids.

If your life was a circus before, it's basically a freak show now.

Excitement was quickly being replaced with fear. I tried to keep my focus on gratitude and just be happy that I was even pregnant at all, but in truth, I was freaking terrified.

I was only about five and a half weeks pregnant when I woke up at 3 a.m. with that familiar and unwelcome feeling. My eyes shot open. I'm pretty sure I said out loud, "Crap, it's starting already," and I plowed my way to the bathroom where I would spend the rest of the night praising the porcelain gods. I couldn't even get up to go back to bed in between puking sessions. I just lay on the cold tile floor and waited for the sun to rise. My ob-gyn had made it clear that I was to call him as soon as I started feeling sick so we could begin the protocol right away. Once we arrived at the doctor's office, we decided to go ahead and do an ultrasound to see what was going on in there. Sure enough, there were two sacs. It was still too early to see heartbeats or even much else at all. I wanted so badly to feel that excitement, the one I'd waited years for. But the sickness was unbearable, and day by day it became more and more debilitating. The medications weren't working; even my doctor seemed surprised and a little confused about it all. Hyperemesis brings a cloud of despair and depression, like a Category 5 hurricane—utter and total destruction. Hopelessness was setting in, and I felt powerless to stop it.

The decision was made that it was time to put me on a round of high-dose steroids. The doctor thought that since steroids have a pretty strong side effect of causing intense hunger, this might be enough to override the nausea and vomiting so I could get some nutrition. After a week of taking the steroids, my doctor was disappointed to hear that I'd still not been able to keep anything down. I'd already lost about twelve pounds in two weeks. So, on January 10, Kennedy's tenth birthday, I was admitted to the hospital where the doctors could work together to figure out how to help me.

Without even the strength to walk at that point, I was wheeled into a large room on the maternity floor. There, the nurse handed me a pink gown to change into and I shuffled my way into the bathroom to change. As I slipped off my clothes, I caught a glimpse of my emaciated body in the mirror. It was worse this time than it had been before, and I could feel the fear of uncertainty creeping in. *Is there anything that can help me? I'm only eight weeks pregnant. How much worse is this going to get?*

Just as I slipped the pink gown over my head I felt another violent churn of my stomach and I dropped to the floor and gripped the toilet for at least the fifteenth time that day. It was like my body was angry, there was nothing left to throw up but that didn't stop my body from trying. As I lay there, I wanted nothing more than to burst into tears and just have a good cry, but tears required some level of hydration that had long since disappeared.

I heard a quiet knock on the door and a new doctor, the one on call at the hospital that day, entered the room. He seemed surprised to find me on the floor of the bathroom and gently helped me get into the bed. We spoke about what to do from here, and while I was let down, I wasn't surprised to hear that they didn't really know what to do. He determined the next best course of action was to put me on an even higher dose of steroids and to give me intravenous fluids for hydration. He thought those two measures would help me get over the "hump," as he put it.

That first day, I did my best to remain hopeful. There was a woman in the room next door to me being monitored for early labor. I lay in bed, listening to the rhythmic sounds of her baby's heartbeat monitor echo through the walls. It was a comforting sound. My babies had little heartbeats, too, nowhere near that strong, but I tried to encourage myself that if I could just get through this, I'd get that big baby belly and hear those loud thumps of their beating hearts soon enough.

The next morning, yet another new doctor came to check on me and see whether I was feeling any better with all the hydration they'd been giving me. Unfortunately, the answer was no. She told me that the Labor and Delivery floor was starting to fill up with women in labor, and since my pregnancy wasn't at a viable stage yet (meaning that if the babies were born they couldn't survive), I would have to be moved. I completely understood and didn't really think the change would make much difference. I figured I'd just be sick as hell in another bed—what did it matter?

Hospital transportation arrived a few moments later with a wheelchair, and we made our way to the elevators. When the door opened and the attendant pushed me in, I asked what floor we would be going to. He quickly replied with the floor number and then told me it was the oncology wing—that was the only place they had an open bed. As we turned the corner toward my room, I felt a sadness in the air. The walls were a dingy tan color, the smell of hospital food permeated the hall, and something just felt off. The feeling in this wing was in stark juxtaposition to the cheerful colors and general sense of hope that seemed to fill the maternity ward.

We entered my room, and the feeling of doom intensified. I'm not trying to get all voodoo witchy woo-woo on you, but the only way I can describe the feeling is to tell you that I felt there was some kind of evil in that room. It felt dark. As I crawled out of my wheelchair to the bed I had an overwhelming sense of hopelessness and despair that I had never felt before. I'd been pregnant and sick before; I'd been in the hospital many times before; but I'd never felt like this.

The first night was okay. CR was able to spend the night in the hospital with me. He'd taken so much time off work already, we couldn't risk him losing his job; so he would stay overnight with me and then head into work first thing in the morning. I could see how awful it made him feel to leave me there, and I kept pushing him to go home and be with our kids. We'd arranged to fly his mom—"Grand Nona," as our kids affectionately call her—out from California to stay at our house with the five kids while CR stayed with me. I'd been in the hospital a few days already, and things were not getting any better. In fact, they were getting worse.

Steroids in very high doses have some really crappy side effects, one of the worst being water retention. It was about day three or four when I woke up and noticed how swollen my arms were getting. The way I was lying, I didn't immediately notice the weight gain anywhere else. I called the nurse and, in a panicked voice, asked her if this was normal. She assured me it was totally normal but warned me that given the dose I was on, the water retention was only going to get worse. I grabbed my phone off the side table and turned the phone's camera on myself. My reflection startled me. My face was so full and round, I almost didn't recognize myself. Again, I wanted to cry, but I knew that tears and emotion would only ignite the violent cycle of vomiting. I lay back into my pillow and stared up at the ceiling. The depression and darkness that already had a small foothold were engulfing me now. Hope was growing more and more distant by the day, and any "light at the end of the tunnel" was dimming fast.

CR had gone home after work to spend some time with the kids and get a good hot shower and a homemade meal. When he returned to the hospital that night, he found me lying in bed, in nearly total darkness, staring at the corner of the room. He approached me slowly and softly touched my leg, asking, "How have you been today, babe? Feeling any better?" I moved my eyes to look at him, but I didn't say anything. I didn't need to. I felt that I had woken up from a dream or something, although I hadn't been asleep at all. That's when I realized that I had been in that exact spot, staring at that exact corner, all day. That was the first time I thought to myself, "I wish I would just die."

The darkness had fully taken over. I saw no more hope, no more light. The voices in my head repeatedly told me that my family would just be better off without me. I'd made everyone miserable, and this was never ever going to end. I was never going to hold these babies, and moreover I was selfish for even wanting them in the first place. Look what I'd done—not just to myself but to everyone I loved.

That was the narrative that played over and over again in my head. It was so loud, it was aggressive, and it was so convincing.

Day after day I'd meet new doctors with new ideas about what to do. One day a new doctor told me that she had done some research and felt that we should try another medication. She said the research looked very promising, and while it wasn't ideal to use meds like this during the first trimester, she was quick to remind me that effects on the babies wouldn't matter if the doctors couldn't keep me alive right now. I was in no frame of mind to make good decisions at this point, and saying yes to her that day will forever be one of my greatest regrets.

The medication did nothing to help my nausea and vomiting, but after a few days of taking it, my despair and depression went from darkness to a total blackout.

I was a shell of my former self, a hollowed-out body whose soul had seemed to go into hiding. I felt nothing. I just stared blankly at the walls and prayed for the Lord to take me from my earthly body.

That earthly body had become unrecognizable to me. By this point, I'd been in the hospital for about a week, and I had retained more than forty pounds of fluid. They had leg compressors going twenty-four hours a day to prevent me from getting a fatal blood clot. My legs were so large I could barely lift them. Ashleigh had to go to the store and buy me new underwear three to four times my usual size and some extra-large men's T-shirts. I had to sleep at an incline because the weight of the fluid on my chest made it hard to breathe if I lay flat, and the fluid in my arms was causing me to have shooting nerve pains down into my hands. My body was flipping out with all these medications, and I began to feel that there would be no coming back from this. I couldn't even remember what it was like to feel good, to feel hungry, to take a deep breath and not want to vomit.

My blood work results came back, and things were getting to a critical point. The doctor said we had to go ahead and put in a PICC line. We'd held off as long as we could. Even though I had done this before in my pregnancy with Shelby, doctors were much more conservative now with placing these central lines, since they don't come without serious risk—the biggest one being the possibility of a blood clot forming on the line. Since the line goes right into your heart, if a clot broke loose and traveled up the line, it would kill you. For obvious reasons, doctors have to make sure the risks are worth the benefits.

Placing this PICC line would allow me to receive TPN, which is a liquid food source that bypasses your stomach and digestive tract altogether and is absorbed directly into your bloodstream. A milky concoction is mixed specifically for you, based on your blood work and your exact deficiencies. Although we had hoped to avoid the PICC line, it seemed this was my last hope.

My line was going to be placed late that night just before midnight. I was alone in my room, CR had gone down to the cafeteria to eat dinner, and I had a rare few moments without nurses and nursing assistants in my room. I literally cried out to God. I begged and I pleaded. I told Him in no uncertain terms, "I need you to come through for me. I need this to work. Please, Father, turn this around for me or just let me die."

Giving God an ultimatum is rarely, if ever, a good idea. I'd like to tell you that I prayed those words in faith that He would help me—but it wasn't faith, it was desperation.

When the time came, all I can really remember is lying on the cold steel table, flat on my back and struggling to breathe. They give you a small amount of local anesthesia where they make the incision for the tubing to go in, but otherwise, you're just awake watching it happen. As the radiologist pushed the tubing up my arm and into my chest cavity, it felt a little like dragging a dull knife across bone. I didn't move or even blink. I was so lifeless at that point that the radiologist probably could have sawed my arm off, and I would have just let her.

She finished up by sewing the line into place on my arm, and even then, as she sewed me up like an old ratty teddy bear, I didn't even wince. The pain was almost comforting. I'd been so numb emotionally for so long, that part of me appreciated the pain to at least know I was still alive.

When the sun rose the next day, it seemed brighter and more cheerful than it had before. I turned my head toward the windows and took a deep breath. That's when I felt it. I hadn't felt it in weeks, and it took me a moment to realize what exactly it was.

Thirst.

I felt thirsty.

Just then my doctor entered the room chatting with the nurse and going over notes as they walked. As he always did, he asked me if I was feeling any better.

A bit baffled, I said, "I'm thirsty."

His eyes rose up from the chart he was reading and met mine with a surprised gaze. "Well, that's great to hear, what do you want?"

I laughed a little and said, "I know this sounds weird, but I want a Diet Coke."

Y'all, the only thing I ever drink is water and coffee. Literally. Okay, margaritas, too, but that's not the point. I never drink soda, ever. I don't even know that I'd ever had a Diet Coke before that. It was the craziest and most bizarre request for me to make, but my body was clearly telling me I needed it.

The doctor laughed and told me I could have whatever the heck I wanted so long as I was drinking something.

About an hour after I drank that Diet Coke, I asked CR to go to the lobby and get me a fruit smoothie. I've never seen the man run so fast to get me a drink!

I was actually freaking keeping something down.

Over the next few days, I was able to keep fluids down—and even some food. The doctors all agreed that I needed to go home. I'd keep the PICC line and the TPN, but I needed to go home and see my babies and rest in my own bed. Even the most medically minded doctors know the best medicine is often being home, with your people.

My body was so swollen that I feared it might actually scare the kids. I made CR take the one and only photo that exists of me from that time and show it to the kids before I came home. I wanted them to be prepared for what Mommy looked like now. The family told me later that Kennedy cried when she saw it. She's an incredibly empathetic child and seeing her mom like that was too much for her young little heart.

The kids all greeted me at the door and then helped me slowly make my way upstairs to my bed. It had been my perch for the difficult weeks leading up to my hospital admission, and it would be my perch for the next couple months while my body tried to recover.

Hyperemesis is a thief. It robs you of so much during your pregnancy and even when it lets up, the damage it leaves behind is long-lasting. Even my teeth have seen the effects of nonstop vomiting for months on end. I'd had a major victory, though—the ability to eat and keep down most of my food meant that I needed the dreaded PICC line only for a month or so, much less time than anyone anticipated. The all-day nausea stuck around for the long haul; I never felt great during my pregnancy. What it means to feel "good" takes on a new definition when you have hyperemesis—it looks a lot more like being able to get around and not throw up all your food.

For as incredibly difficult as this time was, there were still many aspects of pregnancy that I loved. Feeling a baby move inside you is incredible—creepy at times, but mostly incredible. Feeling two babies moving? That's just magic! Well, until they're big enough that the movements err on the painful side, and they seem to be spending the evening practicing for what can only be described as "Baby Fight Club."

We decided to host a gender reveal party for the babies, and we really wanted to involve the other kids since so far this hadn't exactly been a fun pregnancy for them either. We knew they'd love it if we had them spray CR and me with Silly String, either pink or blue, once for Baby A and once for Baby B. My sister and my dear friend Stephanie set it all up; they decorated and made it so special for us, but even that day was not free from the HG monster. I was in the bathroom revisiting my lunch when all the guests arrived, and I just remember praying I didn't puke all over everyone when it was time to do the reveal.

The time came for the reveal, and you would have thought someone handed our kids a fire hose the way they blasted us with Silly String. Much to our surprise, we found out both babies were girls! We were soon going to have five girls and two boys, and I was ecstatic. I think CR felt a twinge of nervousness at the thought of having five daughters, but he was genuinely excited, too.

We loved the idea that the babies were both the same gender. We knew that twins were likely to grow up with a very close bond, and we hoped that the fact that they were both girls would make that bond even tighter. Even though I was growing these sweet girls inside of me, they weren't genetically our children, and we hoped there would be something special for them in seeing physical similarities in each other. Maybe they'd have the same nose, or the same eye color?

The big five, as we like to call the other kids, were all thrilled, too. We wondered whether the boys would be bummed that they were about to be severely outnumbered, but they showed no signs of disappointment. Noah especially, my teddy bear, was overcome with excitement about having not just one but two new babies to snuggle! Jonah was losing his position as the baby in the family, but as we would soon find out, his vivacious and larger-than-life personality needs no particular family position in order to shine.

Kennedy and Shelby were over the moon at the idea of each of them having "their own baby" and started staking claims on which baby, A or B, would belong to each of them. Even Miss Rosie Ru was beaming with excitement over the idea of two new babies. It was hard to tell how much of it all she really understood, but I had a sense of peace that the whole family would do well with this new transition.

Despite everything that happened in the beginning, the extreme sickness, the hospitalization, and the time away from them, my kids were proving to be resilient and understanding far beyond their ages.

19

My Hallelujah Song

Mountaintops are for views and inspiration.
But fruit is grown in the valley.

—Billy Graham

At twenty-eight weeks I went in for a routine doctor visit and an ultrasound. One of the benefits to a twin pregnancy is that you get to check in on your babies quite often, and when you're on the struggle bus every day, these quick peeks at the babies are a saving grace. I loved watching them flip and twist, move their little hands and kick their feet. This was something I could really savor and hold on to during the really rough days. Unfortunately, this particular ultrasound didn't go quite the way I'd hoped.

The first thing they usually look at is each baby's heartbeat. The ultrasound technician found Baby A's heartbeat first, and everything looked great. Then, when she moved onto Baby B, her face changed a bit. She listened a little longer, made some adjustments, and listened again. By that time I'd already figured out there was an irregular beat. The heart sounds would beat in rhythm and then would just skip a few. Even my untrained ears knew that didn't sound right. I tried not to panic as she explained that at this stage, this might not be a big deal at all; the issue could completely fix itself before the baby was even born. But on the flip side, this might be an indication of something really wrong. The ultrasound technician couldn't give me any further answers. She gathered my file and the pictures she'd printed out, then walked me down the hall to meet with my ob-gyn for my regular appointment. I felt a little stunned. I knew it had been too good to be true. There was no way taking all those heavy medications in the first trimester wouldn't have had an effect on the babies. Over and over in my head I blamed myself. *It was all my fault.*

The doctor came in, and she could see the fear on my face. She explained all the same things and scheduled me for a more detailed ultrasound with a specialist. Again, she assured me that most likely everything would work itself out, but I didn't feel any better.

The days of waiting for the next appointment dragged,

although I attempted to keep my spirits up—if not for my own sake, at least for those around me who I knew would worry too much as well. When I finally arrived for the appointment, I was put in the exact same room I'd been in ten years prior for my amniocentesis with Kennedy. This was a déjà vu I would have happily done without. This doctor however, was wonderful. She was from Africa, and if her accent wasn't enough to make me fall in love with her, her gentle and kind bedside manner sealed the deal.

I'm glad I liked her so much, because the news she delivered was hard to hear. She told me that the irregular heartbeat was still there and that she would like me to go see a fetal cardiologist to get a full workup of both babies' hearts. However, her greater concern was something she saw on Baby B's brain—or, rather, didn't see. There was an area at the lower part of the brain that didn't look quite right. She was quite technical in her explanation but all I heard was the possible outcomes. What she saw could be a sign of Down syndrome, it could be nothing at all, or it could be that the baby was missing part of her brain there—with the prognosis for that last possibility being pretty severe. We discussed all the options to dig deeper, but the doctor's recommendation was to keep coming back for regular ultrasounds until the babies were born, and deal with it then. There's not much you can do while a baby is still in utero anyway, so doctors prefer not to do much at this stage if everything else is okay.

I had no idea how to handle this new information. I

wanted to believe everything was going to be fine. I wasn't afraid of the baby having Down syndrome—we'd learned enough by loving Rosie not to be afraid of that—but I was terrified at the third possible outcome. It wasn't even so much the idea that she might never walk or talk, but that she might be robbed of those possibilities because of me.

Even though I knew deep down that the doctors and I made the best decisions we could to keep me and the babies alive those weeks in the hospital, I couldn't help but feel guilty. My stupid body just couldn't handle pregnancy and needed so much help, and now my baby might suffer as a result. I'd prayed and begged and pleaded with God for years to have another baby—now it felt like I was being punished. It's hard to relive these details as I tell this story. I want so badly to be able to tell you that I had complete faith in God, that I trusted He'd protect the baby, or that I handled it all with grace. But I also know I'm a flawed woman. There is no place of darkness so far that He can't reach us, no place of fear or doubt where He can't find us, no ugly side of our sinful nature that He can't redeem.

So there I was, putting on a calm face while the storms of fear and anxiety swirled inside me.

Every appointment that followed revealed the same thing. No change. We'd just have to wait until birth to find out what we were dealing with.

At thirty-five weeks and a few days pregnant, I went in for my regularly scheduled appointment. I was swollen, there were fifty pounds more of me to love, and I was kind of a miserable cow. Hey, it was July in the South, and I was pregnant with twins. I'm sorry, but I just wasn't all sunshine and rainbows. My doctor, who had twins herself, was excellent at being empathetic. She talked to me kind of like a toddler, but I didn't even care. I liked the whole being overly cared for thing.

The doctor looked over the results from the baby's biophysical profile that the ultrasound tech had just done and wasn't too pleased to see Baby A was not doing her practice breathing as she should have been. The doctor was also concerned about fluid levels and some other little markers that weren't quite right. She gave me a cervical check and found I was already four centimeters dilated. I wasn't surprised; there were two babies weighing down on my old, tired cervix. I'm a bit surprised the babies hadn't just fallen out already. I'm kidding—kind of.

My doctor sent me over to the hospital for a few hours of monitoring. She wanted to get a better look at Baby A and make sure we were still okay to keep the babies on the inside.

I got all settled into a triage room, and the doctor came in to check on me. Early on in the pregnancy I had decided that I really wanted to deliver these babies vaginally. I had done so twice before, and I felt confident, as long as the babies were safe, that it was the best thing for all three of us. A few of the doctors had made it very clear that a cesarean section was most likely going to be the outcome, since I was having twins. I spent the rest of the pregnancy praying one of the two doctors I loved would be on call the day I went into labor. I understood that the doctors had their reasons, and that for many moms, caesarean sections are the best option, but I didn't want to dismiss the option of a vaginal delivery if it was at all possible. The doctor entered my room and said, "So, you still think you want to have these babies vaginally?"

I was a bit taken back by his tone, but I insisted, "Yes. Yes, I do."

He informed me that everything would have to be just perfect if I was expecting that to happen and he swiftly left the room. I'd been having steady contractions for hours and I was terrified I was going to end up with an unnecessary c-section because this doctor and I didn't see to eye to eye on what should be done. Perhaps I'm being a tad dramatic, but I'd worked damn hard to get this far with these babies, and with five other kids at home, the last thing I wanted was to be recovering from a major surgery, too.

I rolled to my left, placed my hand on my belly, closed my eyes, and began talking to the babies. I told them that they just needed to chill out, give me another day or two.

I breathed deeply and fell asleep.

An hour or so later, the nurse nudged me awake. The doctor was coming back to check on me and decide whether I should be admitted or not. She mentioned that the monitors might have slid out of place because she wasn't seeing the contractions anymore. The doctor on call came in and checked my cervix for change. There was nothing—all those hours of contracting and I was still at a four. He agreed to let me go home and rest. *Hallelujah*. I quietly thanked the babies and packed my stuff to head home. The nurse was kind enough to give me the doctors' schedules over the next few days so I'd know who was going to be there should I go into labor. My favorite doctor, we'll call her Dr. Awesome, was going to be there the next day, and while I wanted the babies to wait a bit longer to be born, I knew if they were going to come early I wanted Dr. Awesome to deliver them.

My mom had made the four-hour drive from her house to mine just in case the babies made their appearance that day. She wanted to be there to help with our kiddos and whatever else we needed. The next morning she and I were sipping coffee when the phone rang. It was my ob-gyn's office, asking me to come in for a follow-up that day. Apparently the on-call doctor from the day before didn't like what he saw with my blood pressure when he was looking over my chart after he discharged me, and he wanted me to have my pressure checked again. I was feeling a bit off that morning and had even woken up at 3 a.m. with a headache, which was not normal for me. My mom stayed in the car with the kids while I ran into the office for a quick blood pressure check.

Unfortunately, my blood pressure was quite high, and the urine test revealed there was protein present, which could mean I was developing preeclampsia. It's not terribly uncommon in twin pregnancies near the end, so I wasn't overly worried, but the doctor insisted I head back over to the hospital for monitoring again. I don't know what the world was doing nine months prior to this day, but everyone and their dog was in the maternity ward. They had no open rooms, no triage rooms, and even the overflow area was overflowing. My mom dropped me off at the hospital and took the kids home, and CR left work and made his way to the hospital to be with me. I didn't know if this was it or not, but when Dr. Awesome arrived to check in on me, I sent up a few prayers that today would be the day. The midwife who delivered Shelby was even there that day and popped in to check on me. Things just felt right.

I was contracting regularly, and my blood pressure was staying elevated. They wanted to admit me, but I either needed to have another positive urine sample or make more cervical change before they could do anything else. Low and behold, the urine test came back positive for protein, and I was now at six centimeters dilated. I was moved to a labor room and the admission process began—I was having these babies soon! It was almost as if the babies heard someone say it was game on, because my contractions picked up quickly. No sooner did Dr. Awesome finish her cervical exam than my contractions were about two or three minutes apart and quite painful.

There was no need for an induction, these babies were coming all on their own! A small ultrasound machine was brought in to check the positions of the babies, since it's hard to tell with two of them in there. What do you know—Miss Baby B had flipped herself into a breech position. Those buggers had been head down for weeks and now, on delivery day, she decided she wanted go down the slide feet first. Dr. Awesome looked at me and said, "I'll explain all the risks to you, but if you want to try for a vaginal delivery, I'll totally support that."

I could have kissed that woman. I know it makes people nervous, but breech is really a variation of normal—not to mention Baby A was coming out head first to clear the way. She would basically be the fourth baby to come out of there, and she probably could have just walked out.

It was around 1 a.m. when I was ten centimeters dilated and was wheeled back to the operating room for delivery. Even though we weren't doing a c-section, the doctor preferred to deliver twins there just in case an emergency situation developed.

As I lay there on the steel delivery table, bright lights all around me, I closed my eyes and said one final prayer for my babies. I didn't know how our lives were about to change, and whether my fears for Baby B would be proven unnecessary or whether we were heading into a season of extreme challenge. I just didn't know, but I did know that I was about to witness one of God's greatest miracles. Two precious babies were soon to be earthside, and I was going to be a mama again.

Just a few pushes and Baby A, our Ivy Nicole, was born. The doctor held the baby up, and she didn't make a sound—she just stared at us. We still laugh about it now, she was this four-pound little whip of a thing, with a head full of dark hair. I don't think she slept for hours after birth; she just stared at us, as if she wasn't sure we knew what we were doing. Were we even qualified to take care of a baby? She was the most hilariously judgmental newborn I've ever seen.

The nurses whisked her off to get cleaned up just as Dr. Awesome looked me in the eyes and told me to give a big push and we'd get Baby B out. I looked down and saw those tiny little feet and then, in an instant, her whole body was out. The room full of twenty-plus people erupted in cheers. They'd rarely seen a breech delivery, and I could feel how excited everyone was to see it go so smoothly. As they cheered, my whole world went silent. I watched as the doctor wiped off the baby's face and then held her up for me to see, my Baby B, Amelia Jo. I knew the instant I saw her face that all our fears were for nothing. I felt an instant peace. It was as if somehow in meeting her, I was assured that my prayers had been answered in the way I hoped.

The doctors, of course, took her for brain scans and lots of checks by folks more trained and qualified than I, but I was not surprised when they returned her to my room with the news that everything checked out totally fine. Her heart was perfect; her brain was perfect; they couldn't see any of the things they'd seen during our ultrasounds.

The truth is, God's goodness is the same, whether Amelia had been born with abnormalities or not. His goodness doesn't change because of our circumstances. This ending was part of our story, but so were the painful years of infertility, the failed IVF, and the failed adoption. I'm learning, the older I get, how little the ending actually has to do with it all. Whether the outcome had been what we wanted or not, it was the outcome God had for this story, and whether it was to show His strength in creating the miracle in her healing or His abiding love in walking with us through a journey in the neonatal intensive care unit, it's all a part of the greater plan for each one of us. I lovingly refer to Ivy and Amelia as my hallelujah song. Through their pregnancy and birth I learned to praise God in the highs and lows. He never left my side even in the darkest of moments, even when I wasn't sure I'd be able to keep going one more minute.

I left the hospital with arms full of babies, a heart full of gratitude, and a hallelujah song on my lips.

What makes this story even more incredible is that the babies look just like our biological daughters! Amelia looks identical to our oldest daughter, Kennedy, and Ivy has the same curly brown hair and round little face as Shelby. We'd learned all about epigenetics—how just because I carried the babies, the expression of their DNA could change, making them appear more like me. But this went beyond epigenetics for us. This was a clear and profound sign from God that these girls were meant to be with us. Most people assume the twins are our biological children when they see us all out together, and funnily enough, most days I find that I can't tell you which of my kids are biological and which are adopted. They all have expressions, traits, personality quirks, and mannerisms that are just like CR and me. We are their parents, and they are our children—it's really just that simple.

I can't begin to tell you how these two sweet babies have changed our lives. Having twins is a wild ride, and it forced our family to really slow down and be home more. But more important, these babies taught us to savor. We savor the small, seemingly inconsequential moments together. CR and I sit and watch the babies toddle around and play with blocks or dance to their favorite nursery rhymes (and sometimes inappropriate pop music), and we just look at each other in amazement. It's weird to say that your family "needed" a certain child, but in our case, I feel that's the most accurate description. Ivy and Amelia were teaching us a lesson we've clung to since their birth.

Hard isn't always bad.

Having seven kids is hard some days; having twins is hard a lot of days. But it's so incredibly beautiful that the hard gets washed away. People ask us a lot if we think our kids actually like having so many siblings: Do they miss out on anything, or get less attention than other kids?

In some ways I'm sure they do. We can't be in a million places at once, so the kids don't get to do three different sports or have lavish birthday parties. But the fruits I've seen in each of them as the years go on give me assurance that the thing that really matters—the way they love people—is just fine.

Kennedy, our oldest, is wise beyond her years, and I'm so proud of the way she loves her younger siblings. She will be an incredible mom someday, should she choose to have children. We joke all the time that she's better with the twins than I am some days! She struggled with many of the same things I did as a child, and seeing her come out on the other side so much earlier than I did leaves me beaming with pride. She's self-aware in a way that I never was, and seeing her stand in the glory of who she was created to be is the thing I admire most about her.

Shelby is hands down the most compassionate child I've ever met. She sacrifices of herself daily to see that her siblings are happy. She's the first to give up her seat, her toy, or a treat if it means making someone else happy. True, bone-deep compassion is hard to teach, so I take no credit for the trait in her. It's just who she is. Through her actions she shows me what it really looks like to rejoice with those who rejoice and mourn with those who mourn. At just the tender age of ten, she has empathy in a way that I strive to emulate.

Rosie is a light that shines so bright this world can hardly handle her. She's bold and brave in ways I only wish I could be. There is no one she won't give a chance to—she doesn't care how you dress, what you drive, what size pants you wear—there are no qualifiers for her. You are worthy just by being you. I love that about her. She's teaching me to love bolder and bigger than I ever have before.

Noah is tender and strong all at the same time. He forgives faster than the rest of us and gives second chances even when we don't deserve them. He's a musician at heart, and I'm anxious to see what the future holds for him. He was the first child not born to me who called me Mama. He opened my eyes to an entire world that I didn't know before, and he taught me that DNA has nothing to do with love.

Jonah (JJ) is the most full-of-life child I've ever known. His character is just developing, but if the glimpses I see are any indication, he's going to blow us away. He has been the embodiment of joy from such a young age. He has the most incredible laugh, and when he really gets to cackling, you can't help but join him. He's a free spirit in every sense of the word, and he cares little to nothing what others think of him. I think we could all benefit from being a little more like JJ.

Ivy, from the moment she was born, was inquisitive. She bored holes right into my soul with her stare even while she was still tethered to me by her umbilical cord. As a four-pound newborn baby, she'd just lie awake, staring at me as if she had so many questions. As an almost two-year-old now, her personality has changed very little. She's cautious and quiet. You have to earn her trust, but once you have it, she lets it all hang out! Her voice is soft and sweet, and I never tire of watching her sway to the music or apprehensively do the hand motions to "Itsy Bitsy Spider."

Amelia is my wild child. She was easygoing as a newborn, rarely crying or fussing. As she grew into a toddler, we quickly saw her personality change. She's the funniest toddler I've ever seen. She pays attention to what makes people laugh and tries her best to replicate it. Whether it's a funny face or a crazy dance move, she'll try anything! She dances on top of the coffee table and then leaps into thin air, fully trusting that someone will catch her.

Each one of my children is different and unique. They've each shone a light on various parts of my personality that need work, and they continue to mold and change me into the woman I want to be.

I often hear women talk about losing themselves when they have kids and not being able to find the woman they once were. While I do understand, I see motherhood very differently. I'm absolutely not the same woman I was before my kids, and for me that's an incredible gift.

We don't ask the butterfly whether she misses being a caterpillar—the things she could do, or the way her form and figure looked. We marvel at what a stunningly beautiful butterfly she has become. That is what motherhood and adoption have done for me. They have transformed me into someone the old me wouldn't recognize: someone who is unafraid to buck the status quo, unafraid to live outside the box of what I grew up believing was the only way. I'm more empathetic than my younger self, and I have completely new eyes that are eager to see the world. My kids have shown me what it means to die to self, to find joy in the little things in life, and to slow down and savor each day. God used them to strengthen my faith in Him and, through them, my trust in God has found even deeper roots.

I don't long for the days of the old Angie. I needed her

to get to here, just as the butterfly needs the caterpillar to become who she will ultimately be. But I don't want to look back. I want to continue to evolve and to allow Jesus to refine me through my journey of motherhood.

If I could go back in time to give my previous self a message, sure, I could warn myself about the hard times that were coming or caution my younger self about plans that wouldn't pan out or heartbreak that was looming at her doorstep. But instead, I'd like to grab her by the hands, look straight into her eyes, and say, "C'mon girl, this is gonna hurt a little, maybe even a lot at times, but we're breaking free from this box and you're gonna find a life beyond your wildest dreams!"

20

Belonging

For we walk by faith, not by sight.

—2 Corinthians 5:7 (NKJV)

Sometime between when Jonah came home and when we adopted Rosie, I made the decision to start a YouTube channel. I had kept my blog for a number of years, but mostly used it as a way to keep family and friends updated with our growing family. I wanted to create a channel where I could post videos for busy moms about quick makeup, what to pack when traveling with a toddler, homeschooling tips, and anything else that tickled my fancy. My years of running a photography business had taught me a lot about cameras and even some entry-level videography stuff, so this felt like a good next thing to try. My main goal was to stay small and create a genuine audience of people who wanted to build this community with me.

We had begun the adoption process for Rosie in the spring, and by summer I decided to update my subscribers on YouTube with the news. I was surprised by how intrigued people were with the adoption process, so I started mixing in a few adoption-related videos here and there. I'd talk about bonding and attachment, paperwork hurdles, and just the general process as we were going through it. Once Rosie was home, I decided to sit down with her on camera and introduce her to our friends online. We had a few thousand subscribers at the time, mostly friends, family, past clients, and a small but really supportive group of people who'd found my videos. We had built such a sweet bond and sense of community on our channel, which I named This Gathered Nest.

Rosie and I sat down one afternoon and filmed a quick video about how things were going so far and some of the funny things that I didn't want to forget. We told the story about how Rosie used a thin piece of lunch meat at one meal to wipe her face, thinking the meat was some kind of napkin. Or how she shortened the Mandarin word for "dad," which is "Baba," to just "Bob" and went around calling CR "Bob" all day. This was a special video that I knew we'd love to have to look back on, and I had no clue that it was about to change our lives.

About a month after the video was originally posted, I noticed a large spike in views and subscribers. Instead of our channel growing by one or two subscribers a day, we were gaining hundreds and then thousands. Within a few months we had amassed more than 100,000 subscribers and my "Meet Rosie" video had more than a million views. There were, of course, those who were very vocally against our family looking the way it does, but the good news is that, as is mostly true in life, the good far outweighed the bad.

Our video ended up making its way all the way back to China. My inbox was filling up with emails from Chinese people sharing links to newspapers in China that were sharing Rosie's story. The articles shared how an American family had adopted her and that even though she had Down syndrome, she was thriving in this family. The people in China were embracing Rosie in way I could not believe. I have no clue how many people with Down syndrome have even been featured on the cover of newspapers in China, but I'm guessing it's not that many. People were emailing us and telling us how seeing Rosie and her story had changed their perception of Down syndrome. I knew God was doing something really incredible here, and we were simply along for the ride. The growth kept coming, and we found ourselves being featured in magazines and online articles, and I was blown away when the *Today* show came to our home and filmed a segment about our big family!

I feel unworthy of the good things that have happened to us, but I've come to realize that feeling unworthy is actually a good thing. We don't earn our blessings, and we certainly don't deserve them; it's only by His grace that we receive them. I'll do my best to choose gratitude and humility, and I'll hold it all with an open hand.

When the channel started growing, CR and I decided we wanted to share with the world the beauty of adoption, of having a big family, of living life outside the lines of "normal." We wanted to intentionally use the platform to help other children and families across the world. We've seen hundreds of children sponsored through organizations we support. Our community has banded together to raise money for Down syndrome awareness, and thousands of dollars have been donated to orphan care nonprofits we love, such as Mwana Villages, serving vulnerable children in the Congo; Shine Village serving the community in Naminya, Uganda; and of course National Angels, who work on the behalf of the nearly half a million children in US foster care. It's been truly astonishing to watch. Through this journey we've learned so much about ethics in adoption and family preservation, and I love that we can use our platform to help educate people on not just the beauty but also the complexity of adoption.

But the most impactful by far are the emails we receive from families who've decided to pursue adoption, the ones who have decided to check the "yes" box when asked if they were willing to adopt a child with Down syndrome because seeing Rosie made them realize that it's not so scary. Every single time I receive one of these emails or messages, I'm brought to tears. I bow my head and say a humble "thank you" to the Lord for allowing us to be a part of His beautiful story. Hear me when I say that none of this, absolutely none of this, is because we are good, special, or great. Every single bit of our story happened because God is good. He is a loving Father who could do all this on His own if He wanted to, but He chooses to include us—to write us into the story.

The day the twins came from the hospital on my and Rosie's birthday, we worked to find a new routine. While we all loved the overdose of baby snuggles, we struggled through the sleepless nights and the juggling act of keeping everyone on track and in some kind of order. It took months for us to feel like we were getting the hang of raising seven kids, including newborn twins. CR was lucky enough to be able to take three months of paternity leave; when that time was up, we were all so sad to see Daddy go back off to work.

I did my best to manage the long days of homeschooling some kids, doing the school run for others, nursing twins, making meals, keeping the house picked up, and, of course, keeping up with my own job as well.

CR and I would always say that we were better together. Our family was better together. We started talking about and dreaming about what it might be like if he didn't have to work a corporate nine-to-five job. My job was providing me with a full-time income at this point, and we began to consider that perhaps instead of worrying about making more and more and more money, we could learn to live on less.

We knew it was an audacious dream, to have us both be home to contribute to homeschooling, cooking, cleaning, and just the general business of raising seven kids. By now we were fully engulfed by the idea that our lives didn't have to fit inside a box. They didn't need the borders of shoulds, have-tos, or supposed-tos. Our lives didn't need to look like anyone else's; they just needed to go where we felt God leading.

Just after the twins' first birthday, CR and I had a little afternoon lunch date, and we opened the conversation to dream big about what we wanted for our family.

Time together and travel were at the top of both our lists, but we knew in order to make those things happen, we'd need to do some planning, make some sacrifices, and watch for an open door if God provided it. We scratched this all out on paper, planned what we could, and prayed for the rest.

By fall, everything had fallen into place. We sat down one night and went over the list of things we wanted to be in place before we took the leap. They were all there. It was now or never. We saw an open door and went through it, once again saying goodbye to the notion that our lives and even our jobs had to look a certain way. CR left his thirteen-year career in corporate America just a few weeks later, and we never looked back.

We purchased a travel trailer and took the first of many trips that will take us around the US. We call it "roadschooling." Learning about space while visiting NASA, the Civil War by visiting different forts and batteries, the ecosystem via a swampland tour. Roadschooling brings school to life for our kids in a way we had only dreamed of before. We even hope that someday our roadschooling might turn into worldschooling as we travel to different countries and learn about various cultures.

The small amount of travel I've done has literally changed my life; it's opened my eyes to an entire world outside of what I've always known to be true. It has taught me compassion and how to see the world through God's eyes, not through the lens of my American Christianity. My deepest desire is to give that to my kids as early as possible. I want them to skip the Easter morning meltdown and just get right to the heart of it all: loving Jesus and loving His people.

I often think about what my reaction might have been if God had just told me from the beginning what the whole plan was going to look like, what my life was going to look like. I'm pretty sure I would have been terrified and run screaming in the other direction. It's because God cares so deeply for us that He gives us only little glimpses at a time.

Recently, I was discussing with a few friends about how and when we share the full picture of our kids' stories with them—the ones we adopted from hard places, with hard truths that will hurt the kids to hear. My friend Mica said to "think of it like luggage." When kids are toddlers, we give them little backpacks that hold enough of what the kids need but are not too heavy for them to carry. When they go to kindergarten the backpack gets a little bigger; it's able to hold more. By the time you're in college, you have sixteen compartments, and your backpack might weigh more than you do! We give the kids pieces of their stories as they are emotionally ready to carry them, until the day when their hearts can carry the biggest bag, with the full story.

I think God does this same thing for us. He gives us pieces of our story that we can carry at that time, He reveals more and gives us more as we mature spiritually. But don't confuse this idea with the old platitude that I loathe so much: "God will never give you more than you can handle!"

I call bull crap on that. No one can handle with his or her own strength the death of a child, or a cancer diagnosis, or walking through addiction with a loved one. These things go far beyond what we, in our humanness and flesh, can handle. We are meant to lean on God, to fall on our faces in desperate need of Him. We don't handle these things; we open our hands and hand them over to Him.

I'm talking about when God is asking us to step out in faith, to follow Him into a place that feels scary and unknown—to get out of the boat and walk onto the water. Each time I trust Him and exercise that faith muscle, it gets stronger, and I am able to say yes more quickly and step off bigger cliffs as I build that muscle up. As I mature in my spiritual walk with Him, I can carry more in my backpack. I think I want the clarity from God to know what is coming, how it will all turn out—but what I really need is to trust Him more.

I mean, good gravy, when I think back to the weak, fragile, ashamed girl I used to be, I can hardly believe the change. The girl who lived her life to please everyone around her, the girl who was painfully insecure, the girl who just went with the crowd and hoped for the best. She was empty, she was anxious, and she was afraid, even though on paper she had everything you're supposed to want in this life.

God took all the broken pieces of my story and formed them into something new and beautiful that He could use. Not because I'm perfect, but because He is perfect and living within me.

I no longer seek approval from the world about my choices and convictions. The Lord steers this boat, and the only approval I need is His. I've learned to let go of whether people like me or not. Most of the time how other people feel about you has far more to do with them than it does you anyway. People make assumptions based on things like what you drive, how you dress, your hairstyle, and your family size.

I mean, let's get real: I have seven kids and I homeschool. I'm guessing that draws up a visual in your mind that probably includes a denim dress and a three-foot-long braid. But that's not me at all. I love fashion and makeup, I love riding horses, I read only nonfiction, I love Broadway show tunes, I have tattoos, and sometimes I tell inappropriate jokes.

I don't fit in any one box—and, I'm guessing, neither do you. Our souls are made up of a lifetime's worth of experiences, including some that we were too young to even remember but that are locked away in our brains as a reference point for future feelings and reactions. This saying is so true: "There is almost no one you wouldn't love if you knew his or her full story."

My life now is pretty far outside the ideals the world has set before us, and yet I thrive. I put myself out there on the internet for hundreds of thousands of people to see and judge as they please, and yet I'm more sure of myself than ever. My body has carried four babies on the inside, including twins, which has left it farther than ever from this country's version of what is ideal, but this body has rocked seven little ones to sleep and has made its way across oceans to be a soft and loving place for my children to curl up and find belonging. I love this body for allowing me to do all those things. God took this shell of a girl and made her into a strong and formidable daughter of the King!

Every single crack, everything that I thought would break me, made a way for the Lord to exercise His power within me. We'd have no need for a savior if we were perfect with no wounds or broken places that needed healing. We have to stop thinking that life should be perfect and easy all the time. We have to stop selling that lie to our kids. You're never going to be happy all the time; things are not always going to work out how you want them to. God isn't always going to give you what you are asking for. In fact, He tells us in John 16:33 (NIV): "I have told you these things, so that in me you may have peace. In this world you will have trouble. But take heart! I have overcome the world."

God doesn't say we might have trouble—He says we *will* have trouble. We have to learn how to find contentment despite our circumstance. I believe contentment is so hard to find because our "American dream" version of Christianity has lied to us; it has watered down Jesus to a magic man in the sky who gives us whatever we pray for. When that idea proves to be false, we don't know how to handle it. I think back to the faith of those I encountered in Kinshasa. What does that say about God that they love Him and praise Him, yet He's never rained down money upon them? These people barely have what they need to survive. Where do they fit into this prosperity gospel message? We've got to love Jesus enough to trust Him to guide us through the highs and lows, to see it all as part of His greater plan.

I don't have any special knowledge or training, I'm just a follower of Jesus. A woman with more questions than answers. A woman who believes the gospel is meant to be a simple message that's the same whether I live in the West with more than I could ever need or in a mud hut in the villages of Uganda. The gospel is the same. Jesus is the same.

They say you can't appreciate the mountain peaks until you've been on the valley floor. I wouldn't have our twin daughters, Ivy and Amelia, if I hadn't walked through the valley of infertility. I wouldn't have Jonah as my son if I hadn't been through the valley of a failed adoption. Our family might have looked totally different, completely void of the blessing of adoption, if I hadn't suffered in the valley with hyperemesis. Sometimes we just need the pain to experience the fullness of His beautiful story. The most beautiful and valuable jewels in the world are forged in a fire; the only way to remove the impurities is to heat them to a nearly boiling point. I like to say that my children are like my diamond necklace from the Lord, but I'm the one who had to be refined and forged in a fire to get these stunning jewels around my neck.

There are parts of our story that you'll never find in the pages of this book or in a video on our YouTube channel. There are intimate pieces that are meant for only us; but I can assure you, none of my children came to me without a great loss or hardship endured. They've lived through more in their short lives than most of us do in eighty years.

My children are my heroes—the bravest people I've ever known. When people act as if CR and I are special some-how, when people praise us and pat us on the back, I cringe a little. We are the furthest thing from special you could imagine. *We* are the lucky ones; we're the ones who hit the jackpot. We have been gifted seven (so far) of the most in-credible humans you'll ever meet to raise and do our best to love well. We've been given the opportunity to love beyond the borders of our perceived safety, beyond the borders of the American dream. We are merely people who said yes when the open door appeared. There's nothing special or unique about us that made our life what it is. What God does with our yes may be different from what He asks of you, but it's obedience to God that led us here.

As I sit on the sofa, sipping my coffee and watching my children play, I feel fully at peace. I wait expectantly for Jesus to nudge me and ask me to come to the next cliff with Him, to close my eyes and jump with Him. I find myself looking forward to the scary things now, when He is the only answer, the only way I'll get through, when my faith is pushed and stretched; that is when I experience Him so fully. Sometimes I jokingly call myself a "Jesus junkie." At times I have to be careful that I'm truly listening to His callings and not just looking for another cliff to dive off. There's such an incredible rush that comes with following Him into the unknown—a closeness with Him that's hard to find during any other season of life. The closer in line my life gets to cultural norms, the more distant I feel from Him. It's a tricky balance, because Jesus is in the mundane. He is in the everyday tasks, and we don't always have to be moving out in boldness to hear Him. There are seasons for quiet, for calm and everyday minutiae; He is just as present there as He is in the seasons of boldness, countercultural decisions, or bucking the system.

As I type this, I have an email in my inbox from our social worker about beginning to update our home study. CR and I have felt the Lord asking us, yet again, to step out onto the water, because He has something for us. So, we're tackling the mountains of paperwork, opening back up the adoption savings account, and preparing our home and hearts for another little one.

I don't know where our story will end up. Maybe, by the time you read this book, we will have eight children in our home. Maybe we will have endured another failed adoption. I honestly don't know what the future holds, but I know I will rest in the palm of His hand, knowing this story is far from over and feeling immense gratitude for the honor it's been to be included in His redemptive plan not only for my children, but also for me.

The door is open, and we're walking through it once again.

It took me thirty-plus years to learn that the sense of belonging I was so desperately searching for would never be found at the end of a checklist, in a friend group, with a certain job status, or as the result of the approval of anyone at all. My sense of belonging would always be found in Jesus and in owning my story, in finding that what made my life perfectly imperfect was that it was the story God had for me. When I threw away the checklist and said goodbye to the "dream," I found myself.

Good and bad, joy and sorrow, laughter and tears, hope and loss—they are all pieces of the puzzle that is my life. This story belongs to me, and I belong to it.

What I hope you'll take away from this book is my heartfelt plea: if you find yourself running a rat race, unfulfilled and searching, seek Him, and lean in to hear the *kol demama daka*. You'll let go of the fear of being seen as different or weird, of not pleasing everyone in your life. You'll take the risk of being misunderstood—labeled as "too much" or just plain crazy. You'll grab Jesus by the hand and dive off the cliff with Him.

When we see the open door, let's not just walk but *run* through it, with an eager heart and an expectant hope of miracles to come. You never know what could be on the other side. You may just find, as I did, a love without borders and a life you never could have imagined for yourself.

Acknowledgments

For all of you who helped make this dream a reality, I humbly come to you filled up and overflowing with gratitude.

CR, you are my everything. Thank you for being the calm to my storm and the tether to my untamed heart. You've always believed in me, even when I didn't believe in myself. This book never would have been written without you—but more than a book, this beautiful life we've been given wouldn't be what it is today without you. We may never see an empty nest, but I have no fear knowing I walk this road with you by my side.

For my children—I am who I am because of you. You are my greatest accomplishment; nothing I do outside of loving you will ever matter more. I'd lay down my life for each one of you, even though I don't share my candy with you. You've given my life its purpose, and there is quite literally nothing that will ever separate you from my love. You're all brave and kind, and I will always strive to be worthy of the love you so freely give me each and every day.

Mom and Dad, I'm not sure I can find the words. Thank you for believing in me, for supporting me and for loving me even in the times I did nothing to deserve it. You taught me compassion, empathy, strength, perseverance, and to never quit trying. But the single greatest thing you taught me was gratitude: to be grateful for all things, big and small.

To my sisters—you have been my biggest cheerleaders and encouraged me in every step. Sisters are built-in best friends, and I am so very blessed to have you both as mine. You challenge me when I need it and comfort me when I'm broken. I love you both so very much!

For Jennifer—the dream of this book became a reality because of you. Thank you for listening to every single little detail, helping me pull it all together, and ultimately helping this book find its publishing home. You're more than an agent; you're a friend. I am so thankful God crossed our paths.

For Katy and the HarperOne team—you took the pieces of my scattered brain and pulled them together into a beautiful telling of my story. You made me feel like a real writer and helped me to make this book the best it could be. I am eternally grateful you believed in me, my story, and the message we hope the world hears in the pages of this book.

For my friends and family—you all know who you are, too numerous to name one by one. You watched my kids, met me for coffee, accepted hour-long phone calls, waited while I took forever to return a text message, and just generally put up with my foolishness over the past two years, and for that you deserve a flipping medal. Teamwork makes the dream work, and I want to say thank you for being my "Dream Team." My life is so much richer because of each one of you. I love you more than you know.

To our friends from This Gathered Nest—I couldn't say thank-yous without including the hundreds of thousands of you who tune in each week to watch our family. You love us well, support us, and believe in our message. You remind me daily that there is so much goodness in the world. We are grateful to have you as part of our TGN family!

Lastly, but only because I know my words will never suffice, thank you, my heavenly Father. There are tears pouring down my face as I think back to the story You have created in my life—the way You so lovingly rescued me from myself and wrote me into one of Your beautiful love stories. You make beauty from our brokenness. My only prayer in writing this book has been that You would be glorified—that those who read it won't see me, but You living in me. It's all for You, God—for Your glory.

Resources

Over the years we have had the privilege of getting to work alongside so many amazing organizations that are doing the boots-on-the-ground work of keeping families together, providing assistance when needed, and ethically support-ing adoption. These are some of our favorite places to give our time and money to and I'd love to share them with you.

NATIONAL ANGELS
https://www.nationalangels.org

From their website, their mission is clear and simple: "to walk alongside children in the foster care system, as well as their caretakers, by offering consistent support through intentional giving, relationship building, and mentorship. Our long-term vision is that every single child in foster care in the United States will be supported and empowered to succeed."

MWANA VILLAGES
https://www.mwanavillages.org

Mwana Villages is one of the few orphanages with a holistic model of orphan care, serving families and children in Congo. Their model is to prevent orphanhood, pursue reunification first, and seek adoption only when truly needed. They are leading the way in what we believe is a critical time in the landscape of adoption and orphan prevention.

SHINE VILLAGE UGANDA
https://www.shinevillageinitiative.org

I had the privilege of visiting Shine in the spring of 2019. I was blown away by the love poured into everything they do. Shine was born from a simple idea: love your neighbor. Their website states that they are "a holistic ministry that desires to see families thrive in self-sufficiency." Through the community center, empowerment program, teen program, and more, Shine is helping to preserve families, prevent orphans, and proclaim the Gospel.

INTERNATIONAL CHINA CONCERN
https://chinaconcern.org

ICC is near and dear to our hearts, as they are the NGO that took care of our sweet Rosie for the first few years of her life. According to their website, "ICC is a Christian development organization dedicated to changing lives by bringing love, hope and opportunity to China's abandoned and disabled children." They care for the most vulnerable children and seek to end abandonment by "educating and supporting families in raising children with disabilities."

ABIDING LOVE ADOPTIONS
https://abidingloveadopt.com

Abiding Love is an adoption agency like no other; they work only with birth mothers and birth parents, not the adoptive families. From their website, their mission is "to love and support birth mothers throughout the open adoption process." They care for women not just during their pregnancy, but continue to walk alongside birth moms long after placement has occurred, building lasting relationships. They are truly pioneers in the domestic adoption world and we wholeheartedly stand behind their mission.